The Rudolph Factor

The Rudolph Factor

Finding the Bright Lights that Drive Innovation in Your Business

Cyndi Laurin, PhD
Craig Morningstar

WILEY

John Wiley & Sons, Inc.

ISBN 978-0-470-45103-8

Printed in the United States of America.

10 9 8 7 6 5 4 3 2 1

Dedicated to Rudolphs everywhere.
Let your nose glow!

CONTENTS

CONTENTS

ACKNOWLEDGMENTS

We would like to acknowledge the following Boeing Company employees (former and current) for their time, efforts, and contributions to this book. Without their guidance and input, it would not have been possible to accurately describe the transformation and continued journey of the C-17 Program. First and foremost, we thank David Bowman (former C-17 Program manager and current vice president and general manager, Tanker Programs, Integrated Defense Systems at The Boeing Company) for entertaining our book concept and pointing us in the right direction. We also thank Vice President/General Manager Global Mobility Systems, Jean Chamberlin, for her support and allowing us to interview several C-17 employees.

In the Employee Involvement area, we are most grateful to Edward Schaniel; Richard Nicholson, Psy.D.; Charles A. Macias, Psy.D.; and Suzi Hammond-Miller for going far beyond the call of duty to assist us with arranging interviews, sharing many hours of their personal time, and for being Rudolphs! Many thanks to Rick Sanford, Drew Oberbeck, and Craig Savage for their assistance in organizing our visits to the C-17 facility in Long Beach, California.

ACKNOWLEDGMENTS

For their time and contribution in interviews, stories, and quotes, we thank Mark Adams, Leandro M. Aguinaldo, Michael Caldarera, William "Scott" Carnegie, Wayne C. Coleman, P. James Drake, Dr. Katherine "Kathy" Erlick, Ron Gill, Sal Gutierrez, Jake B. Hampton Jr., Elizabeth Haseltine, David Hernandez, Lawrence C. Holzer, Craig Johnson, Bernita Mason, Kami Moghaddam EdD, Anna M. Monaco, Daniel Munoz, Anthony Murray, Don Pitcher, Rosie Robles-Gleason, E. David Spong, Jeff Stagner, Lee Whittington, Patrick Wishall, and Don Woullard.

We also would like to thank some of our non-Boeing Company friends and colleagues for their time in reviewing the manuscript and offering insights and contributions from their own experiences in business and industry, including Steve Lewis, Doug Newton, Katie Peiffer, Steve Shank, and Aad Streng. We'd also like to thank the creator(s) of Skype as it has been a helpful communication tool in our collaborative efforts.

Many thanks to Lisa Ricci for her assistance and time. Last but not least, we are most grateful for the support and encouragement from our literary agent and friend, Stephen Hanselman, and our families. This book project has been a full-time job (in addition to our "normal" jobs) and would not have been possible without them.

Thank you!

C.L. and C.M.

FOREWORD

Here are two forewords by former C-17 Program managers who have gone on to continue great work within The Boeing Company and beyond. The first is written by E. David Spong, who is the current chair of the Malcolm Baldrige Foundation, and the second is written by David Bowman, who is the vice president and general manager, Tanker Programs, Integrated Defense Systems at The Boeing Company.

As one who lived the C-17 journey from early 1991 through the end of 2000, and considers it the highlight of my career in aerospace, I am delighted to provide my commentary on this retelling of the story and the lessons that Cyndi and Craig have so expertly extracted from it!

I am always surprised and intrigued by the differences in the C-17 story as told by various observers. Each person views it through a different knothole or lens and thus can and does make different observations, which, while not contradictory, can appear to tell a different story. For example, one senior member of the Operations (manufacturing) team credited the C-17 success to the implementation of lean. I attribute it to the use of the Baldrige Criteria in driving continuous improvement, and there have been several other variations. The authors attribute it to the "Four Pillars of Organization Greatness" and, of course, the "Rudolphs"!

Since 1998, when the C-17 Program received the Malcolm Baldrige Award, I have studied each of the subsequent organizations that have received the award and observed that what sets them apart is they all have great cultures. Initially, I thought that this was just an interesting by-product of their performance excellence efforts. However, now I believe and know it is a key and necessary element in being a world-class organization. In their research, Cyndi and Craig have brought the idea of culture into greater focus with the identification of the "Rudolph Factor." As one of the leaders on the C-17 Program, we did not set out to create a culture to enable Rudolphs to contribute and flourish. We recognized that it was happening conceptually, and had we been more aware of the cause and effect, maybe we could have done more.

The authors of *The Rudolph Factor* provide a fresh perspective on the factors that contribute to creating and sustaining a high-performing organization. They directly link these factors to the success of the C-17 Program, which they attribute to:

- Progressive leadership
- A team based-culture which leads to innovation
- A steadfast organizational constitution
- An alternative and aligned reward structure

Countless books that provide insight and advice on the subject of leadership are primarily for the *senior* leaders of organizations (not denying that leadership cannot or does not exist at other levels within organizations, but at least not addressing it per se). Cyndi and Craig view leadership with a thoroughly different lens from other researchers by separating it from job titles and positional leadership to those who *demonstrate the commitment to the success of the people around them.*

Many books and articles are also available that detail approaches and techniques to being more innovative, which in many cases seems like trying to solve the old problem of scheduling a breakthrough versus creating, staffing, and funding the equivalent of Bell Labs (where the transistor was invented). The former is probably impossible, and the latter—by today's measures—is prohibitively expensive. Cyndi and Craig's thesis is very different in that they believe and provide evidence to support (based on the C-17 journey) that innovators, or Rudolphs, exist within all organizations when a culture that empowers and enables contribution is created. The authors detail how to achieve this in a way that is easy to use and understand.

The steadfast "Constitution" (which is based on values, rather than rules) is cited as one of the "Four Pillars of Organizational Greatness," which I completely agree with. As the authors point out, it only works well when used in conjunction with the redefinition of leadership.

Last but not least is the awareness that the reward and recognition program must be aligned with the four modes employees operate within—operational/tactical, facilitative/managerial, creative/innovative (where the Rudolphs live!), and strategic/visionary—rather than with the management structure.

I encourage you to read, enjoy, study, and learn from this book, and go forth to identify and empower your Rudolphs to lead you and your organization to world-class results.

E. David Spong
Former Vice President and
Program Manager C-17, and Chair of the
Malcolm Baldrige Foundation

FOREWORD

As an executive on the C-17 Program in the 1990s, I was very much a witness and participant in the turnaround story and enormous breakthrough journey that transpired then and has lived on for over two decades. After a relocation assignment for a few years in Missouri, I had the honor of returning to the C-17 Program to lead it from 2002 through 2007 and then to lead the Global Mobility Systems Division, of which C-17 is a part. I do not believe it is an exaggeration to say that just about everything I have learned about true leadership has come from the past two decades of watching, listening, thinking, and working with world-class people, world-class teams, in a world-class culture.

After receiving the Malcolm Baldrige National Quality Award in 1998, it was no surprise that this organization needed to continue to embrace the Baldrige principles and continue to grow year in and year out (that, in and of itself, is a key recipe for excellence). In 2002, our team received the California Award for Performance Excellence and the Governor's first Productivity Award. On accepting the award, I presented our story to many people at the annual conference, and it was there that I first met Cyndi Laurin. We had a very nice chat (her energy and excitement is very contagious), and she introduced the idea of one day writing a book using our story as a foundation. Needless to say, I was humbled and honored to participate in such a project. And here it is!

Over the years and through all the thick and thin of the C-17 experiences with great leaders like Don Kozlowski and David Spong as well as great USAF customer leaders, I have come to define a very personal definition for leadership that I use as my compass each and every day. That is, that leadership, in its most rudimentary form, is all about, and only about, *connecting people to their future*. Indeed, this is a servanthood definition for leadership, and each word in the definition can be defined further. The C-17 Program story is all about leadership. It took courageous leadership to even attempt the dramatic breakthrough cultural change that occurred, and it took great leadership to assure that disciplined incremental change occurred year in and year out for the past several years.

But the real story is that through strong leadership and a disciplined focus on people and teams (employee involvement and employee engagement), the true *Rudolphs* emerge as is discussed exceptionally well in this book. Rudolphs are not always those obvious entrepreneurs we read about. Rudolphs are you and me. When we are given the right leadership, tools, processes, and enormous latitude (*empowerment*) to find out how talented we truly are and how much more we can contribute than any of us ever thought possible, we can rise to make the impossible possible. We become true change agents!

I hope you enjoy this great book, and I thank Rudolphs Cyndi Laurin and Craig Morningstar for their creative and earnest efforts to share their innovative concepts for us to learn and to apply. The Rudolph factor as explained in this book is indeed replicable anywhere. One last thing I can assure you from experience—the journey is more fun than you can possibly imagine. Why else do it?

David M. Bowman
Vice President and General Manager,
Tanker Programs Integrated Defense Systems,
The Boeing Company

Note: The views expressed in this Foreword are my own personal views and not those of The Boeing Company.

PREFACE

The Boeing Company has a long tradition of financial success by providing exceptional products and services to its many customers. However, it has also suffered—along with many of its competitors and suppliers—from the cyclic nature of the commercial aircraft business with wild swings in the demand for new aircraft. In the late 1990s, the dramatic increase in aircraft orders was negatively impacting its ability to deliver quality aircraft on time. In addition, the integration of Rockwell, and later, McDonnell Douglas with the heritage portions of Boeing was causing headaches, to say the very least. Airbus was proving to be a tough competitor, leading Boeing both in market share, new orders, and on-time deliveries. The Boeing Company seemed unable to define or offer a new commercial aircraft that met industry needs.

The company was also plagued by adversarial relationships, poor performance, and a loss of focus that was exacerbated by post-9/11 market pressures. Suddenly, at the lowest point, while experiencing cultural decay, market pressures, and the serious financial consequences they wrought, Boeing found its bearings and maneuvered a remarkable turnaround in record-breaking time that placed its rivals on the competitive ropes.

At the core of this impressive reversal of fortune are some crucial lessons Boeing learned a decade ago about innovation with its widely lauded cargo aircraft called the C-17 Globemaster. We believe these are lessons that Boeing is building on today enterprise-wide in several other Boeing facilities. While the technical elements and capabilities of the C-17 aircraft surpassed all expectations, the organization was not performing well. In an effort to stay alive, the customer (the U.S. Air Force), along with C-17 management and the employees partnered to fix the Program that unleashed a massive, cultural revolution.

In the simplest of terms, a new way of looking at leadership and progressive practices involving employees are the cornerstones on the path to Boeing's successes. The C-17 transformation story has become the proverbial "pebble in the pond" and has influenced change at other Boeing sites and within other companies, such as Parker Hannifin and American Airlines.

In 2007, The Boeing Company and the U.S. Air Force granted us unique, sole-authorized access for the purpose of writing this book. Our intention is to use The Boeing Company's successful transformation as a platform for teaching organizations how to elicit and benefit from creative, revolutionary innovations from within—from their current employees. Several aspects make this story unique. First and foremost, *The Rudolph Factor* principles are transferable to and replicable by any type or size of organization in any industry. At its core, the C-17 story reflects a revolution of the Program's business culture that was riddled with adverse and antagonistic relationships and facing potential cancellation, but that went on to align nearly 10,000 employees to a common purpose and was subsequently awarded our nation's prestigious Malcolm Baldrige National Quality Award, which is presented by the president of the United States. President Clinton, who presented the Award to the C-17 Program in 1999, referred to it as a "National Treasure."

While the rate of this significant transformation was quite impressive (approximately six years), the thinking underlying the methods is even more compelling. A shift in thinking took place that drove new actions and behaviors and produced (and continue to produce) phenomenal results. The Boeing C-17 Program's success is based on progressive leadership; the development of a highly participatory team-based culture; a steadfast organizational constitution; and an alternative, aligned reward structure. Above all, this nontraditional creative and innovative thinking occurred in what could be considered one of the most highly regulated and historically bureaucratic environments. We believe the tenets underlying the Boeing C-17 Program have been successfully transplanted and are currently in the process of being implemented into several other Divisions and Programs within The Boeing Company.

In the first section (Chapter 1), we explore general problems companies face with regard to eliciting innovative thinking from employees and how this lack of involvement and contribution goes hand in hand with disparate, disconnected, and/or dysfunctional corporate cultures. Combined, these nontangible issues diminish possibilities for an organization to be a world-class leader, and more importantly, to have any notable competitive advantage.

The second section (Chapters 2 through 4) explores lessons learned and demonstrates how the leaders of Boeing's C-17 Program recognized Employee Involvement and the development of a culture of creative contribution as the two most important factors in revolutionizing their business culture—as gleaned from their experiences in identifying, nurturing, and building their own *Rudolph Factor* (a term referring to a small percentage of every company's highly creative and unconventional thinkers). Boeing C-17's success can be correlated to examples from other companies that have orchestrated innovative thinking and experienced transformative results as well. The primary lessons are grouped into three stages—each of which builds on the progressive and innovative thinking behind the C-17's success. The first stage reveals the methods of identifying Rudolphs (Chapter 3, "Why Rudolph, You Ask?"). The second stage explores how companies who have become adept at identifying their Rudolphs must then learn the lessons of "Nurturing Rudolphs to Maximize Their Innovative Contributions" (Chapter 4).

The third and final section of the book (Chapters 5 through the Epilogue) demonstrates how "Establishing a Rudolph Culture" (Chapter 5) *without* addressing three other vital areas of the organization will not result in organizational greatness. We share ideas of how to integrate a highly innovative Rudolph Culture with three other essential elements of organizational dynamics, which combined make up what we refer to as *The Four Pillars of Organizational Greatness*. The Four Pillars include the following:

1. Establishing a Rudolph Culture
2. Redefining leadership as "connecting people to *their* future"
3. Developing a Corporate Constitution—an unwavering institutional memory and infrastructure that does not change no matter who is leading or what external circumstances are presented
4. Creating an Aligned Reward Structure—consonant with different types of employees (worker, manager, Rudolph, or executive) and in alignment with the other three pillars

The beauty of *The Rudolph Factor* is that it often *does not require a company to use or spend additional money or resources* because Rudolphs are already there—they only languish in not being identified, nurtured, or having a healthy system from which they can effectively contribute. This book is intended to be used as a tool to assist people within organizations to get on the same page and to facilitate enterprise-wide cultural transformations. The design and content are structured as an ongoing reference guide for employees, managers, executives, and of course, Rudolphs! The process of transforming the culture, redefining leadership, creating a "Corporate Constitution," and aligning the reward structure becomes a company's sustainable competitive advantage and a powerful mechanism for leveraging *The Rudolph Factor*.

Enjoy!

CHAPTER 1

THE PREVAILING FORM OF BUSINESS CULTURES

A company without competitive advantage is as good as extinct; and in today's global economy, the fundamental elements of competitive advantage have changed. While the uniqueness of a product's features (function, design, quality, and/or price) was once considered the primary criteria for an organization's competitive advantage, today's criteria are comprised of nontangible features that are more *people-based* rather than *product-* or *process-based*. This is not to say the products or processes are not important. We are simply referring to the notion that a people-centric focus has a profound and positive effect on the products and processes people manage.

Currently, companies tend to be product-only or process-only focused (people tend to be left out of the equation altogether). The ability to leverage an organization's *Rudolph Factor* begins with this fundamental shift in thinking, which then provides management with a new approach to catalyzing the creativity in its own ranks as developed from the winning ideas and tools proven in the crucible of one of the world's largest companies—The Boeing Company.

In our work with businesses large and small, we have recognized that roughly 10 percent of any organization's people are *true* agents of innovation—people who can shine the light exactly where a company needs to go to achieve higher levels of innovation. This critical 10 percent of an organization is its Rudolph Factor—borrowing a metaphor from the famous reindeer of the popular children's Christmas story, *Rudolph, the Red-Nosed Reindeer.* As the story goes, Rudolph's bright, illuminated nose led Santa's sleigh through the fog to accomplish its mission of delivering toys all over the world by Christmas morning. Similarly, modern day Rudolphs in the business world tend to go unnoticed until their unique and unconventional thinking is needed. Companies like Boeing that have learned to identify, nurture, and leverage their Rudolph Factor are today's leaders of innovation and change, and hence, dominate their respective fields with this unique and *sustainable* competitive advantage. It is sustainable over time and through external circumstances because people-centric organizations are far more difficult (if not impossible) to replicate versus product-only or process-only focused organizations.

Another element of today's global competitive environment requires management to balance time and resources in addressing efficiency and innovation. Most business innovations are generally related to greater internal efficiencies and improvements within the various organizational functions. From a management perspective, efficiencies are typically perceived as internal issues, while innovations are considered external or growth initiatives. The most serious limiting factor that managers face in achieving performance excellence is the lack of employee engagement and creative contribution as it relates to problem solving, performance management, process improvement, as well as growth and expansion efforts. Furthermore, significant percentages of the workforce are ambivalent, if not discontent, with the vision and culture of their respective organizations. This can be seen by the prevalent lack of contribution and involvement by employees. More tangibly, it can be measured in absenteeism, lateness, safety issues, a decrease in productivity, an increase in waste or scrap, an increase in defects, rework, or poor service among many other process- and performance-based issues.

There are a myriad of problems with regard to eliciting creative and innovative thinking from employees and managers. In considering employee contributions, some managers may not recognize a winning idea when presented with it because it may not always be terribly clear what innovative thinking looks like. To compound the problem, the command-and-control style of management continue to be prevalent in many organizations. This prolific style of management has been around since the dawn of the industrial age and causes many employees to mentally *check out* because the message sent is that employees' ideas, thinking, and intellectual contributions are not valued nor appreciated. It is the "we pay you to work, not to think" syndrome. Even though there have been hundreds of articles and books written about how ineffective command-and-control management is in a business environment, it continues to be popular among many of today's organizations. For people and organizations interested in being world-class engines of innovation, management style (overt as well as covert) is an extremely important element to examine. Senior leadership and management must look at the means by which they elicit performance from their employees—is it facilitative and supportive or threatening and controlling? Generally speaking, the structure by which employees are rewarded or penalized sheds ample light on the style of management practiced.

To address issues related to innovation, many organizations direct a significant amount of time and resources to *fix* the symptoms of employee ambivalence, rather than focusing on the underlying motivators and the organizational structure driving the lack of engagement and creative contribution. Some companies have gone so far as to require their employees to take intensive psychological assessments to identify who might be true agents of change—those employees we refer to as *Rudolphs*.

Other times, managers create extravagant employee suggestion programs to wrangle inventive and innovative ideas—only to stifle the process when it comes to implementation. It does not take long for employees to stop contributing altogether when their ideas do not fit within the organization's collective paradigm. Managers desire innovative and inventive thinking and many times do not know how to manage the associated risk that comes with innovation. Instead, they try to control it when they should be fostering it. There is a big difference between managing and controlling risk, and many managers are uncomfortable with innovation because the perceived risk might put them in an unfavorable light if the innovation fails. This is not by intention—managers do not set out to sabotage innovative thinking. Managers tend to operate within the parameters of the structure and system that have been created for them. So, rather than going out on a limb, managers attempt to control and limit innovative contributions from workers, thus killing creativity and employee engagement altogether.

AN ALTERNATIVE IS AVAILABLE

By creating an environment where innovative and inventive thinking can flourish, today's progressive managers are producing new ways for employees to become more involved. Historically, Employee Involvement (EI) has been included as part of "Corporate Outreach Strategies." When researching various EI programs, we found that many EI programs were primarily focused on charitable giving programs, employee volunteerism, and workplace giving. These types of EI programs are not what transformed The Boeing Company's C-17 Program. While there is distinct value in charitable giving and volunteerism, the level of EI we are referring to is more accurately defined as *employee engagement*. The Boeing Company and a handful of other very large companies, like Royal Philips Electronics (Philips), Toyota, and the Ricoh Group are aware of and recognize the value in engaging people on a grand scale.

Leading the Employee Involvement (EI) initiative was one of the most challenging assignments of my career, and it turned out to be the most rewarding experience of organizational and personal transformation that I could ever imagine. What seemed like a *project* became a labor of love with results that exceeded my wildest expectations and continue to leave a legacy beyond today for all the leaders and employees who are part of the journey.

McDonnell Douglas Corporation veteran leader, Don Kozlowski, came to Long Beach in the early 1990s to lead the turnaround of the C-17 program. He partnered with our USAF customer and exceptional leader, General Ron Kadish, and both began collaborating with the United Auto Workers (UAW). McDonnell Douglas (now Boeing) was transforming the organization and focusing on partnership, quality, and process management. Kozlowski asked me to lead the initiative to engage the workforce through EI. Employee Involvement would be the vehicle and culture to drive decision making from the lowest levels to improve productivity, innovation, and employee and customer satisfaction. It would be a true partnership between all stakeholders.

My most amazing observation has been seeing people working together to improve the business when the appropriate environment is established. The Rudolphs naturally step forward, and I believe that everyone has a little bit of Rudolph in them. "The Magic is in the People" is a phrase that caught on when the teams began showcasing exceptional results. With this, the *spirit* permeates throughout the organization and creates a unique pride of ownership. My advice for leaders is to empower your people and get out of the way! You won't be sorry.

I am very honored to have been part of the C-17 transformation. I credit its success to the workforce members, who are the real heroes, who made it happen and continue to reach new heights each year.

Ed Schaniel
Former Director of Employee Involvement (Retired),
The Boeing Company

Aligning employee engagement with the corporate vision and strategies is a significant contributor to a progressive company's business success in any industry. For employee engagement to be a powerful, driving force for innovation, responsibility (and control) must be turned over to employees (along with a supportive structure and systems identified here). This concept of handing over responsibility to employees flies in the face of the prevalent command-and-control style of management. If reading this is making you a bit nervous, remember to recognize that handing over responsibility and control involves more than simply passing the baton to the workers. As you will learn, it requires a shift in awareness, thinking, and actions from senior leadership as well as a newly defined role for high- and mid-level managers. It also requires a close organizational examination—and generally, a modification—of the culture and reward structure. In some cases, as with Boeing's C-17 Program, it required an entire business cultural revolution.

The value of shifting responsibility and control to employees is far greater than maintaining the current way organizations have been doing things. Shifting responsibility to workers does *not imply freedom of action*, where anyone can do whatever they please. It refers to having a voice and an avenue to implement ideas, which naturally compels employees to *voluntarily* take on innovative and creative thinking above and beyond their current responsibilities. Progressive managers have altered their role to that of advocate for employee engagement and have absolutely relinquished the means of control they once used (or their perception/illusion of control) to allow more ideas to percolate from the ground up. In the case of Boeing, leadership created entirely new positions to support the area of employee engagement at a corporate-enterprise level as evidenced in the language of many current job descriptions, which include training in EI as one of the hiring criteria.

An article by Nancy Lockwood in the March 2007 issue of *HRMagazine* reports that engaged employees "do a better job, are prepared to go the extra mile, deliver outstanding performance, and see opportunities to lead others."* Findings also include that employees with the highest level of commitment perform 20 percent better and are 87 percent less likely to leave their organizations, all of which points to a clear link between employee engagement and bottom-line business performance. The Boeing C-17 Program's internal EI Practitioners provided us with several graphs and data indicating a positive, direct correlation between employee satisfaction indices and employee engagement initiatives.

A PSYCHOLOGY OF CHANGE MODEL — *AVTAR*

Before you can appreciate the type of transformative results experienced by Boeing's C-17 Program, it will be

---

* Nancy Lockwood, "Leveraging Employee for Competitive Advantage," *HRMagazine* 52, no. 3 (March 2007), 1–11.

most helpful to understand the context and framework of how that program developed its Rudolph Factor. It is also important to note that while experimentation was responsible for much of what transpired, we have clearly identified the thinking behind the C-17 Program's tenets of success so that your organization can gain a sustainable competitive advantage through leveraging your own Rudolph Factor via *intentional design*, rather than through *trial and error*. The most significant characteristic of Boeing C-17 Program's successful transformation and incredible financial results is directly related to the level of employee engagement that was built using creative and innovative thinking and contributions led by their Rudolphs.

We define employee engagement as those workers who deeply care about the future of their organization, who voluntarily choose to invest extra effort, who respect (and live) their organization's values, and who see a line of sight between their personal future and the organization's mission and vision. Over the past three years, studies have indicated that engaged employees are more customer focused, effective team players, stay longer, have fewer safety issues, and have a profound effect on financial business performance. *The 2008 Employee Engagement Report* by BlessingWhite revealed "fewer than one in three employees are fully engaged in their jobs [in the United States], and 19 percent are actually disengaged."*

---

* BlessingWhite. *The 2008 Employee Engagement Report*. Princeton, NJ: BlessingWhite, Inc. www.blessingwhite.com/eee__report.asp.

Recognize that a substantial amount of untapped potential for improvement exists right now within your own organization! Operating at one-third of total power is like running on less than three cylinders when you have a powerful V8 engine. While operating at 33 percent might get you slow, forward movement on flat ground, consider how the same engine performs when going uphill. Mediocre. Running an organization at 33 percent is not acceptable in today's highly competitive, global markets.

One of the elements that makes the Boeing C-17 story unique is not necessarily the initiatives and strategies they implemented. These are easy to find and available to any organization. Rather, it is the awareness and value placed on people that led to a highly engaged, team-based Rudolph Culture. We created a model to assist managers in their responsibility of facilitating the psychology of change with employees. As we all know, change is the only constant in organizational life. We refer to our psychology of change model as AVTAR, which is an acronym identifying the five stages required to enable participative change. Change, or transformation, will not occur unless each stage is realized in a linear form. For a manager to inspire employees to embrace change, they must provide and facilitate the following:

1. *Awareness:* The manager is responsible for generating awareness of the proposed change.
2. *Value in awareness:* The manager is also responsible for providing employees with supportive

information that will inspire them to find value in the proposed change. What is unique about our model is that you cannot go on to the next step until *employees truly find value in the change*. In other words, there is a *shared responsibility* in this step, and if employees do not see the value for themselves, you will be imposing change (which is the antithesis of creating a Rudolph Culture).

3. *Thinking:* While the manager still has some responsibility in supporting the thinking of employees in this stage, this is the stage where *employees begin to bear the burden of responsibility for the proposed change.* If you are the manager, and you do not begin to see a transfer of responsibility taking place with a noticeable shift in thinking by employees, you must go back to stage two. Often, managers must let go of their own agendas and put themselves in the shoes of their employees. This is done by asking employees thought-provoking questions, exploring their frame of reference, and working to enhance it with additional information and insight. This is not a time to put band-aids on problems, nor is it a time to give lip service to employees and trick them into buying into the proposed change. If managers do not buy into the value and thinking of the proposed change, then employees will not buy it either. As you can see, stage two is critical. You will begin to see everything change

in stage three as employees start asking questions reflecting their new awareness. If managers do not know the answers to the questions raised, they will have to find them. Many answers will be discovered together. Employees must feel 100 percent confident that the proposed change is in their best interest and in the best interest of the organization or you will not get the level of engagement found within Boeing C-17 and other successful organizations.

4. *Actions:* In this stage, responsibility has mostly shifted to employees. The beauty of this process is that thinking drives actions, so the shift in thinking that takes place literally sets the stage for new actions and behaviors. Again, if you are not seeing actions and behaviors supporting the desired change, you must go back to stage two. It is simply a clear indication that employees do not see value in the proposed change and that the right mix of information has not yet been shared or presented.

5. *Results:* The results are everybody's responsibility. For the proposed change to be embraced and realized within an organization, the results will be a natural outcome of the shift in thinking and new actions and behaviors. If the manager is continuing to force results with reward and punishment, once again, step two was not clearly manifested in the AVTAR process.

As you can see, the most significant stage, and the most difficult to complete, is stage two (finding value in your awareness). Boeing's C-17 Program, Toyota, Ricoh Group, and Royal Philips Electronics all share the same secret of continued success. Their awareness (A) of people being their competitive advantage and the value (V) placed in that awareness inspired and shifted the executive leadership and management's thinking (T). Every action (A) and decision made is based on this shift in thinking, driving highly impressive results (R). At Boeing's C-17 Program, these results continue over a decade later.

For the AVTAR tool to be effective, we have some fundamental principles driving our model. First and foremost, we do not believe that employees *naturally* resist change. If employees know why a proposed change is necessary and what it entails (and it brings improved conditions to their lives), they will support it 100 percent. They will become advocates of the change, and the results will speak for themselves. Furthermore, we believe change can and does occur on its own, but there is no guarantee the results will be tied to desired expectations. Managers need tools to effectively facilitate change, and while there are many tools that address change in the areas of action and results, there are very few that address it in the areas we are suggesting—at the hearts of senior leaders, managers, and your employees.

Awareness and value in awareness can be found at the deepest levels of personal and organizational change. Without value discovered through new awareness, nothing really changes—people may understand change at an intellectual level but not *feel* it enough to compel further thoughts or actions that could create sustainable business results. For example, we are all aware that smoking cigarettes is bad for our health; but it is only when people who smoke find value in their awareness that smoking is bad for their health that the idea of quitting (or not starting) is a possibility. After the value in your awareness is realized, you cannot help but think differently. It is like a light switch has been turned on or the proverbial "ah-ha" moment. Life is never the same after an epiphany.

As noted previously, much of the responsibility in the AVTAR process is with the manager, and from the value (V) to the thinking stage (T), a shared responsibility is formed. At this point, the responsibility for a proposed change—while still shared—shifts more to the employees than managers. When used effectively, the manager does not have to continue to prompt the employees on what to do because the employees now see it for themselves. This point of the process is generally recognizable when the employees begin asking for more information. Again, the results (R) are a *natural outcome* of appropriate and effective thinking and actions. The story that follows is a great example of what it looks like to go from raising awareness to finding value in new awareness.

It was one of those dreaded meetings. You look up at the chart and see *red*, and you know the news is

(*continued*)

(*continued*)

not good. Red means failure. This meeting was about employee involvement (EI)—this wonderful, engaging concept that empowers employees to tap into their full potential. Yet the chart was screaming red. Employee involvement is an organizational goal, yet it truly appeared to be more of a burden to some teams. Filling out forms, hosting meetings, creating team-based business improvements, preparing for empowerments, agendas, meeting minutes, action items, and blah blah blah. . . .

People felt they were too busy getting *real* work done. They did not have time for EI. As a result, teams were performing red to the goal, and EI was in jeopardy of falling by the wayside. I sat in the meeting completely baffled. I thought to myself, "The people must not know the true power of EI." A quote from Lily Tomlin immediately entered my thoughts, *"Somebody should do something about that."* Then I realized I am somebody. So . . . I raised my hand and volunteered to create an improvement process. The teams were scattered in various locations, and we had two months to accomplish what usually takes a year to do. With a pen in one hand and a chocolate bar in the other, I began scribbling down my thoughts.

I sat down with my manager. He liked my ideas and strategy, and we created the EI road show. You know . . . the kind of road show like musicians do when they want everyone to hear their music. They write a bunch of songs, then hit the road and start singing. That's what we did (minus the singing). I created and assembled EI binders for each group including tabs for team charter, empowerment plans, and Team-Based Business Improvement (TBBIs). The binders took what seemed to be this overwhelming EI task and put it into perspective by sorting it into smaller tasks. The road show also included conducting a kickoff meeting with each group to get them started on their EI journey and to influence their thinking so they could clearly realize the benefits of EI.

Now let me tell ya. . . . I thought this was going to be so much fun, but what I initially encountered was comparable to performers getting tomatoes thrown at them from the audience. These people did not want to hear what I was saying. They did not share my views about empowerment. They literally battled me during the entire one and a half hour presentation. As I dodged the multiple comments flying in at me from all angles, another quote came to mind, "When life hands you lemons, make lemonade." The more they protested, the more I knew I had to stay. That was one of the most memorable one and a half hours I have ever invested in the lives of other people.

I witnessed firsthand the transformation of people's thinking—the true power of influence. As I explained how EI was their tool to having their voices heard, a few

(continued)

(*continued*)

people began to lean forward and listen. I explained how EI provided the platform for them to get visibility for *their* ideas, *their* projects . . . a few more leaned forward and listened. In the final moments of the meeting, the tone shifted from "why we don't want EI" to "so . . . how would we do this?" or "how would we do that?" I knew they were starting to get it. EI is the employee's tool to help each other and help themselves. To this day, that same team holds the record for performing up to the EI goal. They outperform all my other teams. They actively apply EI to create solutions, achieve goals, and to influence others. They even volunteer to do extra EI exercises. Now that is EI at its best!

The EI road show delivered results. All teams closed the year not just meeting the EI Vision Support Plan (VSP) goal but exceeding the goal! We recognized the need for our teammates to realize the value and benefits of EI. The attempted *change* was in perceptions. EI is not a burden but the answer to overcoming burdens. When EI is in effect and being practiced, it actually creates a positive work environment, which in turn encourages employees to be more productive. Overall, we wanted to build confidence, boost morale, develop leadership skills, and enhance the bottom line by educating our teammates with EI principles.

Anna M. Monaco
Employee Involvement Team Lead Focal—Supplier Management, The Boeing Company

As previously mentioned, there are a handful of other companies deeply entrenched in employee engagement, and this can be seen in the language used in the company's vision, mission, and value statements. For example, one guiding principle at Toyota is to "Foster a corporate culture that enhances individual creativity and teamwork value, while honoring mutual trust and respect between labor and management." As it relates to employee engagement, this particular underlying philosophy is one of the secrets to the financial success of the company and is captured through each individual's creativity, contributions, and effective teamwork. As a result, Toyota encourages and fosters personal growth for its employees; and its employees are deeply committed to Toyota's successful future. It is a natural win-win for long-term business success and for employees. What could be better?

Another example is from the Ricoh Group. Their management philosophy is to "constantly create new value for the world at the interface of people and information." The underlying principles that set the foundation for management's actions and decision making are:

- Think like an entrepreneur—be a Rudolph (entrepreneurs create their own business around their ideas, while Rudolphs prefer to be employed by someone else).
- Put yourself in the other person's place.

- Find personal value in your work—to be actively engaged.

Underlying philosophies and principles in the form of vision, mission, and value statements can be found on most company web sites. The proof, however, is in the pudding—through actions, business results, and employee satisfaction levels. To achieve organizational greatness with a Rudolph culture, business results cannot come at the cost of employee satisfaction.

Our last example is Royal Philips Electronics whose "Vision 2010" works to further position the company as a people-centric and market-driven organization with strategies and structures reflecting the needs of their customers, while also increasing value to the shareholders. Management at Philips fully recognizes the value of engagement and has generated an enterprise-wide engagement strategy to ensure its alignment with contributions from shareholders, customers, and employees. As with the other companies mentioned, these philosophies and guiding principles noted are not devoid of assessment. Each company has a well-established, comprehensive set of metrics and a continuous improvement system supporting their underlying, people-focused tenets.

Boeing's C-17 Program leaders discovered that their impetus for change—and basic survival—would depend on getting their employees involved and contributing at a *soul* level. As you will read in the next chapter, before their transformation, the concepts around EI would have been nothing short of a miracle. The level of employee frustration, hostility, and cultural dysfunction could not have been any worse. Yet, through the fog, senior leadership's fundamental thinking was that EI would drive innovation and sustain the Program's cultural transformation. To this end, senior leaders and management resigned their former practice of stopping one initiative or effort and starting a new one and moved to an alternative way of thinking that built individual efforts into a collective journey.

Each of the companies previously noted recognize that to have employees who are fully engaged in their work and committed to the success of the organization, cultural transformation must be viewed as a journey—not as an event with a distinct beginning and end. With Boeing's C-17 Program, the driving philosophy continues to be that *everything begins and ends with the customer*. This thinking is essential to the continued success of the Program and is spreading across The Boeing Company and to many of its suppliers and customers. In everything from the development of the vision, values, and goals; to conducting internal assessments, managing leadership systems, creating EI teams that are supported with productivity improvement tools; and to integrating a systems-improvement process—the customer is *always* a part of the equation.

Customers are your most important reason for what you do. Everything is based on your customer's requirements, customer commitments, and the customer's strategic imperatives. Relationships are as important as the technical aspects in business. We have found that by constantly working on the social behaviors, our output of product and/or service is greatly enhanced. As changes occur, one of the biggest challenges in a team-based culture is becoming flexible in our thinking, our actions, and habits and in how we approach our work. To help our teams in this area, we conducted training classes on topics such as holding effective meetings, communication basics, handling team conflict, customer/supplier relations, and we taught teams how to use the basic problem-solving tools. There were approximately 30 training themes we applied in this training effort. The training covered both the socio as well as technical aspects to our business.

We also helped teams identify their strengths using the SWOT analysis model (Strengths, Weaknesses, Opportunities, and Threats). This strategic tool can be used at all levels of the organization in designing the strategic plan. The last thing I will mention is also helping the teams identify their vision and mission statement and their team's charter as it relates to their work scope. When the entire team has a grasp of what's in it for me (WIIFM), and they respect and trust one another, business results start becoming a reality. The key is to continue to press forward and make adjustments along the way as required, and to make everything you do a win-win situation.

Charles A. Macias, Psy.D.
Employee Involvement Practitioner, The Boeing Company

Chapter 1 Review

- Tools and initiatives come and go, but *people* are what make the tools work.

- A command-and-control style of management kills creativity and innovation.

- Employee involvement and engagement must be aligned to the vision and business strategies.

- Responsibility and control must shift to the employees.

- AVTAR is an effective model to facilitate the psychology of personal and organizational change and is a critical tool to building a Rudolph Culture.

THE BOEING COMPANY AND THE IMPETUS FOR A CULTURAL REVOLUTION

There are relatively few companies that value and encourage the contributions of their Rudolphs. However, The Boeing Company is one such company. Because of this company's sheer size and scope, it might be helpful to first learn a little bit about Boeing's operations. According to the Census Bureau, there are approximately 900 companies in the United States with over 10,000 employees; and as one of the largest companies in the world, The Boeing Company is also one of the most complex.

As with any formidably sized company, Boeing has its share of award-winning areas and those that can benefit from improvement.

The Boeing Company is the world's leading aerospace company. It employs over 160,000 people in 70 countries around the world and generated revenues of $66.4 billion in 2007. It is considered one of the largest U.S. exporters in terms of sales. It has two main business units, *Boeing Commercial Airplanes* and *Boeing Integrated Defense Systems (IDS)*. There are approximately 12,000 Boeing commercial jetliners in use today, which translates to roughly 75 percent of the entire global fleet of commercial aircraft. In addition to its impressive commercial base, the IDS Unit provides air-, land-, sea-, and space-based platforms for global military, government, and commercial customers, including NASA's international space station.

The Boeing Company has a long history of world-class leadership and innovation. For the purposes of this story, we are focusing predominantly on an IDS-based Program that manufactures the Boeing C-17 Globemaster, which is a highly innovative cargo aircraft used for military and, more recently, humanitarian efforts.

"FORTY AND NO MORE!"

In 1992, Boeing's C-17 Program was near the brink of cancellation with a threat to reduce its initial order from 120 to 40. The statement, "Forty and No More!" reverberated throughout the Boeing C-17 facility and became their burning platform—or the impetus for their cultural revolution. Plastered on banners for all to see read the words, "40 and No More. . . . Unless You Perform." For the Boeing C-17 Program to survive, all 10,000 employees would have to do more than just participate. All individuals would have to be deeply engaged in the process of transforming their culture to the same standards of excellence they demanded for their product. Every employee would need to rethink his or her commitment to the Program.

Some of the specific problems contributing to the potential cancellation of the Program included a highly adversarial relationship between the customer (U.S. Air Force) and the United Auto Workers (UAW) and among the employees. We heard a number of stories of political maneuvering, derailing, sidelining, and sabotage. It was nothing short of a toxic environment. There were also several quality problems, cost overruns, and late deliveries—compounding a lack of confidence from all constituents.

In addition to "Forty and no more," another slogan heard repeatedly throughout their cultural revolution was "*Change* management, or change *management*." Managers would have to change their thinking, or they would be let go. To date, we do not believe there has been another transformation similar to the Boeing C-17 Program in terms of size and scope with the level of regulation and inherent bureaucracy, for a program that, at the time, had just one customer—the U.S. Government.

It is more than a stroke of luck that the executive team realized it would take more than improving processes to survive. Leadership's ability to identify, nurture, and leverage their Rudolph Factor—wrangle their Rudolphs—was a significant contributor to transforming from a highly dysfunctional culture to an award-winning organization. After their cultural revolution, the Boeing C-17 Program delighted the customer in that they were able to deliver on or ahead of schedule with record quality in place. They also began to receive recognition from their customer for excellent service. Subsequently, they were able to reduce the price by 25 percent for a follow-up order of 60 additional aircraft. These phenomenal results led to more customers, more aircraft orders, and within a six-year time frame, became the model acquisition program for the U.S. Air Force and a lucrative program for the largest aerospace company in the world. Their accomplishments were manifested and recognized by receiving the prestigious Malcolm Baldrige National Quality Award presented by the President of the United States in 1998. In 2003, the support arm of the C-17 Program, now part of the Aerospace Support Division of Boeing, also received the Baldrige Award. The Baldrige Award is the highest award given by the U.S. Government for Quality.

So, how did they do it? You might be expecting us to say leadership, quality assurance, teamwork, vision, strategy, and so on. Well, it might surprise you to learn that it was a shift in *thinking* that influenced leadership's decisions, quality assurance tools, and initiatives, and simply thinking about how they were thinking that took them so far. We believe thinking about how one thinks results in outstanding results!

Before you can realize similar results and generate greatness in your own organization, you have to recognize and appreciate what the Boeing C-17 leadership's shift in thinking entailed and how it influenced actions, behaviors, and results. We firmly believe that one organization cannot emulate the success of another by simply doing what the other is doing. From the AVTAR model introduced in Chapter 1, attempting to copy another organization's success generally only encompasses actions (A) and results (R). We know it requires delving into deeper waters to understand the awareness (A), assess the value in that awareness (V), and thinking (T) to drive all actions (A) and decisions contributing to their success (results; R).

When any organization—no matter how big or small—undergoes a cultural revolution, it requires far more than strategic planning exercises, generating mission statements and visions and posting them on the wall, and certainly more than imposing process- and performance-based initiatives on employees. While those have value, it also takes *heart*, meaning it takes an emotional investment by everyone involved to pull it off. Any truly great organization looks beyond satisfied stakeholders to include an engaged workforce, engaged customers, and engaged stakeholders. There is an emotive connection when employees are engaged that cannot and does not exist otherwise.

If you read articles about Boeing C-17's transformation or another company that has transformed from mediocre to exceptional, you are likely to find a very tactical path of actions that resulted in more profits, reduced waste—or in Boeing C-17's case, was awarded the Baldrige Award. Most corporate transformations read something like this: "We first formed a committee to assess where we currently were. We formed teams for problem solving, teams for quality assurance initiatives, and teams to keep an eye on other teams. We brought in consultants . . . and more consultants, and implemented JIT, TQM, TPS, ISO, Six Sigma, Lean, 5S, Kanban, Balanced Scorecard, Appreciative Inquiry, PMI . . . and . . . and . . . and . . . built strategies around each . . . "

While we are being a bit facetious with regard to the description and acronyms noted in the previous paragraph, we do agree that there is immense value in process improvement and performance management tools. However, imposing initiatives and tools upon employees says nothing about the compelling reason they are being used. In other words, managers are leaving out the whys behind the hows. Only when employees understand the whys can they effectively perform the hows. Unfortunately, the most priceless information you can learn from another company's best practice or through benchmarking is what you cannot see, measure, or control! Secrets to success are found in the collective awareness of the current state of affairs, and they include everything related to processes and products, as well as what is happening with the people—their perceptions and thoughts about how the strategies fit into the larger scheme of things.

Consider how change and new initiatives have been implemented in your organization. Are the people around you engaged and creative or ambivalent, discontented, and disengaged? What is the collective thinking of the organization? Does anyone ask, "Why are we doing this?" How would you describe the current management style? Will the organization's culture support a revolution of thinking and behaviors? Does the organization's structure support a cultural revolution? Does the current reward structure encourage the kind of thinking and behaviors that will be necessary during a cultural revolution once the organization is entrenched in the process?

Anyone can copy the strategies and initiatives, purchase the same equipment, build a similar facility, and replicate most processes and products . . . but emulating a culture and style of leadership as well as emulating philosophies and principles that generate creative and innovative thinking is the secret to organizational greatness. Your Rudolphs hold the key for unlocking the door to get your organization there. They have the uncanny ability to propagate a new way of thinking and behaving—a new culture—throughout an organization. The following story points out how culture, leadership, and underlying driving principles can start at the grass-roots level as they did in the C-17 Program.

I believe that all people are motivated by two things: to know that their opinion counts and that they can make a difference. My experience has shown that when asked genuinely, most people want to be involved in positive change, and that can improve the entire company. Even though the desperate situation of the C-17 Program created a case for change, it was not obvious how to fix it. The moment of desperation is not the best time to start experimenting with fixes, so I recommend that organizations not wait until they are in trouble. It could have been too late for the C-17. I have realized that there are many factors that made it successful, including persistence with a business model, always improving the approach based on feedback, and never wavering in commitment to the core values and business imperatives.

One of the most effective approaches for replication was to build a community of change agents across the company regardless of where they were in their journey. As with so many things we tried, we did not know if it would work well or not; but we had a philosophy that ongoing collaboration among stakeholders is good. We asked other business units if they wanted to be involved in learning new ways to improve their business on a totally voluntary basis. We asked them to identify "focal points"—people who were interested in organizational improvement. *Now we were tapping into the passions and intellectual capital of the people (the Rudolphs).*

In a few short years, we had a herd of over 500 Rudolphs from various business units, at all levels, interested in employee involvement for business results. Some were part-time, some were full-time, and some were just interested. They finally had a voice and a support system. We held regular conference calls, shared best practices, and held internal conferences inviting key leaders to share their encouragement and motivation. It was truly a grassroots approach. Leaders who were ready built it into their business plans and goals. No matter what happened organizationally, you could not stop the force of the people. Even with a whole new set of leaders, it is still in effect today and continuing to grow at a corporate level across this mammoth company.

Richard Nicholson, Psy.D.
Employee Involvement Practitioner, The Boeing Company

THE RUDOLPH FACTOR

As mentioned in Chapter 1, we believe that Rudolphs, whose main intention is to improve their organization through involuntary creative and innovative thinking, by leveraging their ability to affect change, and by taking action, make up approximately 10 percent of every organization. In other words, their most creative and innovative thinking—their Rudolph space—is their work environment. They can turn on their creative juices (i.e., illuminate their nose) in the blink of an eye, but they cannot turn it off. Rather than turning it off, most Rudolphs will redirect their creativity elsewhere (outside of the organization) if it is not embraced or supported by their management, culture, or reward structure.

The modern day Rudolphs we share with you are involuntary, passionate, and creative contributors to The Boeing Company. They connect the dots that others do not see, meaning they have a unique ability to perceive several contributing variables in any situation. From this ability, they tend to identify causes of problems (rather than symptoms of problems) and generate solutions more quickly and efficiently than their counterparts. Before the introduction of the Rudolph language to people at Boeing C-17, Rudolph-types were referred to as "Practitioners." In other organizations, they have historically been labeled as *change agents, square pegs, radicals, misfits, loose cannons, zealots, mavericks, heroes, entrapreneurs, or innovators*—among other names. Has anyone ever called you names or not let you play in any reindeer games? Based on this limited description, do you consider yourself to be a Rudolph? Can you think of anyone around you who fits the mold?

Rudolphs played—and continue to play—a tremendous role in Boeing's story, within the Boeing C-17

Program and beyond. But it is not just the Rudolph Factor that has sustained the Program's results over the past 10 years. It includes the successful integration of a Rudolph Culture with a progressive, new way of looking at leadership, the creation of a Corporate Constitution, and an alignment of a reward structure that encourages and sustains their very unique competitive advantage—these four elements we refer to as the "Four Pillars of Organizational Greatness" (see Figure 2.1). As noted in Figure 2.1, the strength and integration of the Four Pillars of Organizational Greatness is dependent upon all five parts of the cycle, including actions, behaviors, and outcomes that are

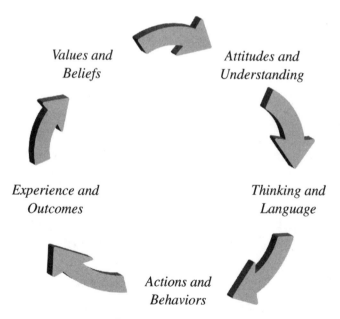

Values and Beliefs

Attitudes and Understanding

Experience and Outcomes

Thinking and Language

Actions and Behaviors

Figure 2.1 Four Pillars of Organizational Greatness

observable and measurable as well as those things we cannot see (values, beliefs, attitudes, understandings, and thinking). You must look beyond the actions, behaviors, and outcomes to recognize that Boeing C-17's success is transferable and replicable to any size organization in any industry.

GENERATING A PEOPLE-CENTRIC VISION

The Boeing Company's Vision 2016 is "People working together as a global enterprise for aerospace leadership." Boeing connects and protects people globally. You can easily access their strategies, core competencies, and values on their web site—as you can with most organizations. Within the Boeing C-17 Program Vision, there are eight values supporting a people-centric focus (again, as opposed to a product- or process-centric focus). In finding the bright lights that will drive innovation in your business, focusing primarily on people—with secondary focus going to processes and products—is an essential element. Before you can start identifying and nurturing your Rudolphs and build a Rudolph Culture, you must first address the values and belief systems (real and perceived) that drive your organization's collective attitudes and understanding.

If Figure 2.1 was illustrated as an iceberg, we would not be able to see, measure, or control anything under the water, which would include the values, beliefs, attitudes, understanding, and thinking. However, above the water we find language, actions, behaviors, and outcomes—all of which are tangible characteristics. Again, most organizations operate above the water, in the realm of measuring, managing, controlling, rewarding, and punishing anything that they can see and measure, leaving the most powerful and influential elements out of the equation. If you are able to tap into the wealth of power that lies under the water (in our iceberg analogy), then you are well on your way to organizational greatness. The beauty of it is that it is not terribly difficult ... it starts with an open mind and communication.

In the next three chapters, we are going to shift gears from prevalent thinking styles and practices that have only worked marginally to a highly progressive way of thinking and operating. Our intention is to first raise your awareness (A) and inspire the corresponding value to your awareness (V). This process should provoke shifts in your current thinking (T). With AVT in place, it will be up to you to select the appropriate actions (A) to get the results (R) you desire. With regard to results, we are striving for more companies to achieve sustainable organizational greatness through leveraging their Rudolph Factor as a competitive advantage.

In defining organizational greatness, there are three distinct elements, all of which must be present: (1) an extraordinary product and/or service, (2) treating all people associated with the organization (customers, employees, suppliers, etc.) *impeccably* well, and (3) a vision that goes far beyond the boundaries of the organization. While many companies have been successful at achieving one of the three elements, there are not very many that have achieved two, and even fewer that have all three in place. Unfortunately, for those companies that have an extraordinary product or service—it can come at the cost of treating people poorly. This is primarily due to the prevalence of product- and process-focused cultures, rather than cultures that are people-centric. When people are treated impeccably well, the products and processes they manage will tend to follow suit and perform exceptionally well.

In the next chapter, we offer tools and strategies from Boeing employees as examples of how to start identifying your Rudolphs and nurturing them (not to be confused with rewarding them, which is addressed in Chapter 8), and building a team-based Rudolph Culture. Let us begin by introducing you to the wonderful world of Rudolphs and a glowing new way of thinking.

Chapter 2 Review

- In the Boeing C-17 story, necessity drove invention (Forty and no more!). For other progressive companies, a desire to achieve performance excellence has been equally compelling.
- *Change* management, or change *management*.

- When it comes to the psychology of change, what you cannot see has the greatest value to the organization (beliefs, values, attitudes, understanding, and thinking).

- A people-centric focus is a must for sustainable business success.

- An extraordinary product and/or service must work in conjunction with treating people impeccably well.

WHY RUDOLPH, YOU ASK?

In 1939, Dartmouth graduate Robert May published the beloved children's Christmas tale titled *Rudolph, the Red-Nosed Reindeer* as an assignment from his employer, Montgomery Ward. Apparently, Mr. May had a track record of creating catchy children's stories and jingles, so he was charged with the task. As we understand it, he contemplated several different names before choosing "Rudolph." Mr. May had a very young daughter named Barbara, and unfortunately, while working on the story, his wife Evelyn was dying of cancer.

In the first year of its release, Montgomery Ward gave away 2.4 million copies of *Rudolph, the Red-Nosed Reindeer.* People everywhere loved the story and could easily relate to Rudolph having to overcome many obstacles to triumph in the end. Everyone loves it when the underdog wins! With the onset of World War II, the U.S. Government instituted paper rationing. Even though the number of copies distributed decreased during the war, by 1946, nearly six million copies had been sold. Interestingly, Robert May did not receive royalties for his huge success because his employer owned the copyright. As it happened, he was deeply in debt as a result of enormous medical expenses from his late wife's illness. In 1947, the CEO of Montgomery Ward, Sewell Avery, transferred the copyright to Robert May, and he and his daughter were able to reap the benefits of its success for several decades. While Mr. May took a short break from Montgomery Ward in 1951, he returned and stayed until his retirement in 1971. He passed away five years later in 1976. Whether he ever fully recognized the enormity of his contribution to global Christmas lore is not known.

We believe Robert May's intention was to create a unique character that was something of an outcast among his peers. But once recognized for his signature illuminated nose, Rudolph rose above his challenges and contributed to the success of Santa's mission to deliver gifts around the world by Christmas morning. Rudolph's personal challenges, unique talents, and ultimate success could have been inspired by May's personal experiences; it has been reported that he had to endure teasing during his childhood years because of his small stature. Yet he, himself, went on to overcome his challenges and contributed to the birth of a global folklore and Christmas hero.

Why Rudolph, You Ask?

As it happens, Rudolph's journey from an outsider to a hero parallels the career tracks of many of today's out-of-the-box, creative and innovative thinkers—the critical 10 percent of every organization that makes up the Rudolph Factor.

MODERN DAY RUDOLPHS

You may be wondering how *Rudolph, the Red-Nosed Reindeer* relates to the business world. In our work with organizations large and small, we have noticed that there always seems to be a small percentage of employees that are highly creative and innovative, yet they may not really fit within their organization's culture. They have shared many exciting, innovative ideas with us—as well as stories of frustration in not being able to voice or implement their ideas in their work environment. We used to refer to these people as "creative, entrapreneurial, out-of-the-box thinkers who do not really fit very well in their organizations." After many conversations among ourselves, we realized this description was a bit long-winded and that we needed to come up with an easier (and shorter) descriptor. We did not like the traditional descriptor of *entrapreneur* because we discovered these types of people were far more complex than an employee of a large corporation who thinks like an entrepreneur. One day, it struck us like a bolt of lightning. They are sort of like Rudolph, the Red-Nosed Reindeer! While they do not run around with red noses, they do have a different way of thinking than those around them.

Rudolphs in the business world are filled with "bright" ideas, but they tend to be considered either heroes or outcasts by those around them, depending on the corporate climate at the moment. Interestingly, in the Christmas fairy tale, Rudolph was also considered to be an outcast by his peers until a critical moment—the eleventh hour on Christmas Eve—at which point he was hailed the hero for saving Christmas for all of the boys and girls around the world. Under the right circumstances Rudolphs are appreciated, but for the most part, they are ignored. Needless to say, the Rudolph metaphor stuck with us . . . as did the thought of having a red nose versus a brown one.

We became rather fascinated with the notion of Rudolphs in the workplace. Although we come from very different backgrounds (Cyndi comes from the academic realm, and Craig comes from the corporate and entrepreneurial worlds), our thoughts and experiences branded us as Rudolphs. We also shared similar experiences with other Rudolphs who had faced obstacles like we had in our previous work environments. We decided to test our theories—as any good academician would do—and find an organization with a successful herd of Rudolphs. We searched and searched and found more and more Rudolphs but struggled to find organizations that recognized and leveraged their innovative thinking on an ongoing, systemic basis. It was not like we could call a company's corporate headquarters and inquire about their Rudolphs!

So we decided to survey people we thought were Rudolphs within our own circles. We quickly learned that in almost every case, employers were not aware of the latent creativity of these employees (Rudolphs). However, the employers that did nurture their Rudolphs benefited tremendously and tended to leverage their innovative thinking and problem solving as a significant sustainable competitive advantage. We expanded our informal research to include people we did not know through online business networks, such as LinkedIn. We posed a number of questions and found even more Rudolphs. Along this journey of learning about Rudolphs—and being Rudolphs ourselves—we have come to recognize that managers who successfully nurture their Rudolphs are leaders in their industries.

After learning about Rudolphs and the value they bring to organizations, most people ask, "How do I find them?" There are five different ways to identify Rudolphs including:

1. Self-assessment
2. Senior manager recognizing Rudolphness in a peer, manager, or frontline worker
3. Middle-manager recognizing it in a peer or subordinate

4. Peers recognizing it within their group or characteristics of it in their manager

5. An employee involvement or engagement program

An example of a program that elicits creativity and innovations is Boeing C-17's Creative Edge Program. We share further details of how it works in Chapter 5, "Establishing a Team-Based Rudolph Culture." All five avenues act as a funnel for identifying Rudolphs (Figure 3.1). As you read about Rudolphs in the work environment, you might recognize Rudolphness in yourself and you may be able to easily spot other Rudolph friends, family members, or coworkers you know. If not, do not despair. We also share a comprehensive list of how to identify your bright lights that will drive innovation in your organization.

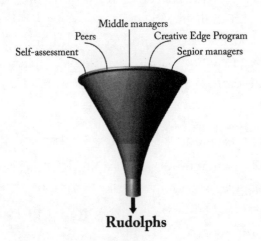

Figure 3.1 Rudolph Funnel

When people read about Rudolphs, there is a natural tendency to ask, "Am I a Rudolph?" In interviewing a variety of people within Boeing, we would share characteristics of Rudolphs, and for some, the light bulb literally turned on right before our eyes (pun intended). They would say, "That's *me*! I really want to fit in but just don't." Before we get into the characteristics, our disclaimer is that it is not all glory to be a Rudolph. In fact, most Rudolphs we interviewed shared more stories of being mistreated or becoming targets at work rather than being the heroes of the herd. Many have been conditioned to "put mud on their noses" and not contribute anymore because their managers, culture, or reward structure do not support their creative and innovative thinking.

If your curiosity is getting the best of you, Table 3.1 offers a short survey to analyze whether you might be a Rudolph in your work environment. Remember, this is not a scientific assessment; it is simply a short set of questions to help you determine if your nose is aglow.

If you check "yes" on a majority of these questions, you might be a Rudolph. If these questions do not make any sense to you or do not resonate with you, then you most likely are not. Remember, every organization is made up of approximately 10 percent Rudolphs, so it is reasonable to assume there is a one in ten chance that you will identify yourself as a Rudolph.

There is nothing good or bad, right or wrong, special or not special about being a Rudolph. And we are certainly not saying that Rudolphs should have any special

Table 3.1 Rudolph Self-Assessment Survey

Please check yes or no for the following 10 questions	Yes	No
1. Do you find yourself thinking about ways to solve problems or make improvements at work when you are not at work?		
2. Do you tend to see the potential in your organization—see opportunities for improvements or solutions to problems that those around you do not see?		
3. Are you sometimes referred to as a change agent, maverick, loose cannon, troublemaker, innovator, genius, hero, scapegoat, or similar names?		
4. Do you feel as though your thinking is different from the people around you, and do you have difficulty fitting in?		
5. Do you often ask why things are done a certain way?		
6. Do you consider yourself entrepreneurial even though you work for an organization?		
7. Do you discover unconventional ways of implementing your ideas just because you know they will be of benefit to the organization?		
8. Do you find inspiration in doing things that make the organization better?		
9. Have you ever said to yourself, "If my manager only knew how good I could make him (or her) look?"		
10. Have you ever said to yourself, "Why doesn't my manager leverage my ideas?"		

privileges that others do not have or that they should be separated from the herd in any way. However, if you are a Rudolph, then you will need to learn some tools to be more effective from where you are within your organization. If you are not a Rudolph, it is in your best interest to learn how to find, support, and leverage their naturally creative and innovative thinking. Remember, part of what constitutes a Rudolph is that they want to make others and the organization look good. Seriously, they are most driven and interested in win-wins. Personal gain is not a primary priority for a genuine Rudolph.

For those of you who do not feel like you are a Rudolph, here are some other characteristics you can use to identify them in your work environment:

- First and foremost, Rudolphs are naturally creative and innovative thinkers. Some Rudolphs may appear a bit eccentric to the people around them.
- Rudolphs generally share unconventional ways to solve problems and have an easier time than most at identifying the root cause of a problem. They will express frustration at putting band-aids on symptoms of problems. They like to get their hands (or hooves) dirty when it comes to problem solving.
- Rudolphs involuntarily spend an average of four to six hours per day (outside their normal workday) thinking about new ways of doing things, or simply making things better for their organizations.

- Rudolphs are passionate about their work and *light up* when talking about their role or a particular project they are working on. You can tell they are excited when the pace of their speech increases, they use quite a bit more gesturing, and their eyes are bright (almost twinkling).

- They often ask "Why?" even when it is not the most popular question to be asking, which can make people around them feel uncomfortable.

- They tend to challenge the status quo because they believe questioning it is of value and benefit to the organization. Challenging the status quo is also how they discover what they need in order to solve a problem. It may appear as if they are trying to rock the boat just for the sake of rocking the boat, but that generally is not the case with Rudolphs.

- Rudolphs see their world through a lens of possibility, opportunity, and potential. This is the driving motivation behind their involuntary, creative, and innovative thinking. Often times, the opportunities presented are nontraditional or unconventional in nature.

- Rudolphs do not have the intention of self-promotion—in other words, their actions are not based on climbing corporate ladders. They certainly appreciate being recognized—even promoted—for their work, but it is not the primary motivation for their actions.

- They also tend to easily connect the dots that others do not see. In other words, they have the ability to quickly synthesize many variables to solve problems or make improvements. It may appear to non-Rudolphs as if their ideas come out of the blue or that there is no rhyme or reason behind their thinking. When this occurs, question Rudolphs to clarify or further explain their thought process.

- Rudolphs have a greater awareness of dynamic systems than non-Rudolphs. They tend to be natural systems thinkers and see the whole forest rather than a single tree ... or just the bark on the tree. They may express frustration if people around them are having conversations about the bark, rather than the forest.

- They do not want to be an entrepreneur or run their own business; however, they think like one. In some cases, for their own mental and emotional well-being, some Rudolphs will leave their organization and start their own business because the organizational work environment can take its toll on their enthusiasm and natural creative thinking.

- Rudolphs prefer to leverage the name, reputation, resources, etc. of an organization, rather than starting and managing their own businesses, which would take time away from being creative and innovative.

- Rudolphs prefer collaborating with others versus *going it alone*—although many may appear as loners to non-Rudolphs because they have chosen to not play the game.

- They have the ability—and at the very minimum, the confidence—to turn their ideas into action. If they feel they do not have the appropriate skills, they will do whatever is necessary to gain the abilities to manifest their innovative ideas/solutions into reality.

- They act on their ideas, sometimes without knowing how they will accomplish them. You might hear a Rudolph say, "It can be done—I don't know how—but I can see it." The *how* is always revealed in time.

- Rudolphs rarely rely on convention to put their ideas into action. They tend to appear like trailblazers, troublemakers, or loose cannons to non-Rudolphs.

Whether you are a Rudolph in your work environment or not, we believe everyone has a little Rudolph in them—that little spark or twinkle in the eye everyone gets when talking about his or her passion. Whether or not the nose is aglow depends on the context of a situation and the environment. When you are in your Rudolph space, it is similar to being *in the zone*—you have little awareness of time passing, and you can see nothing but potential and opportunity around you. Because of this intense passion, Rudolphs tend to make leaps in their fields of study or hobby of interest, and some actually go so far as to revolutionize concepts, organizations, environments, or entire industries.

Many inventors, change agents, and problem solvers are Rudolphs. However, as previously mentioned, there are distinct differences between being an entrepreneur and a Rudolph. Both are highly creative but have different skill sets. For example, a friend of ours who works at Disneyland engineers and builds roller coasters. If he were an entrepreneur, he would leave Disneyland to start his own rollercoaster-building company. He would be responsible for all aspects of his business, from the creative design to raising capital, hiring workers, sales, marketing, quality control, transportation, and so on. He is a Rudolph because as much as he loves the creative work, he also loves being able to leverage his employment at the "happiest place on Earth" to do things that he could not do as an independent rollercoaster manufacturer. Although an entrepreneur would love to create and build a product or service and build a company to support that creativity, our friend has no desire to raise capital, hire people, or run a business.

Another friend of ours is a Rudolph in the education realm, working for a large university, because she is deeply passionate about facilitating the learning process in others. She has no desire to start her own education or training business, and she enjoys leveraging the name and reputation of her university to gain access to all kinds

of behind-the-scene grand tours of manufacturing facilities and other unique opportunities to gather ideas. If she
were an independent trainer or contractor, these types of
invitations would not be so readily granted.

Our last example is a software developer and Rudolph
that we interviewed named Steve Lewis. When asked if
the characteristics of a Rudolph resonated with him, he
responded by saying,

That's me exactly—a creative guy in the Information
Technology industry that [unfortunately] generally
scares the heck out of people. I have always been
willing to take risks in the various positions I have
held in companies, trying different ways to do things,
and so on. Most of corporate America sees me as a
liability rather than an asset. The few managers who
have recognized my talents and creative thinking were
rewarded with reliability of software, substantial cost
savings, and the ability to expand their businesses.
I have to admit, though, that managing my career
has been tough. I take positions that sound interesting and pray that my manager understands me. Or as
my resume once said, "Give me enough rope to hang
myself"—meaning, give me just enough freedom to be
able to do something revolutionary. Most employers
don't even know where the rope is. I've been called
crazy, nuts, and genius a few times as I pursue a
path less traveled. In the end—when the project is
completed successfully—I am the hero for a day.

While Rudolphness may differ based on context, circumstance, and environment, one constant for all Rudolphs is that they cannot help but spend time (1) involuntarily thinking about the things they are most passionate about, (2) acquiring the capabilities to manifest their thoughts into reality, and (3) taking action. In the business realm, after many interviews with all different types of employees including frontline workers, managers, executives—and the Rudolphs sprinkled throughout those roles—we had an epiphany. We discovered that, generally speaking, we could determine which mode employees were in by simply measuring what percentage of time outside of their normal eight-hour workday they spent involuntarily thinking about their work (Table 3.2).

Table 3.2 Rudolphs and Time Spent Involuntarily Thinking about Work Outside of a Normal Eight-Hour Workday

Percentage	Hours	Mode	Rudolphs
0–25	0–2	Tactical/operational	
26–50	2–4	Facilitative/managerial	
51–75	**4–6**	**Creative/innovative**	**Yes**
76–100	6–8	Visionary/strategic	

Based on a handful of relatively simple questions and listening to the language people used, we are able to determine if an employee is tactical, managerial, strategic, or innovative. It is important to note that the mode does not necessarily correlate to the title of the person's position—unless someone has recently added "Rudolph" to the traditional organizational chart.

Again, to be reasonable, this does not mean that every person who thinks about work for an additional six to eight hours a day is a Rudolph; but, that characteristic would certainly lead us to more investigation. The number is simply a reflection of the percentage of time spent involuntarily thinking about work. It is also important to note that everybody works within all four modes as shown in Figure 3.1; each mode coming to light under different circumstances or in different types of environments. Our goal is to locate those people whose *Rudolph space* is located in their work environment and to nurture their thinking so that they can bring an ongoing steady stream of creativity and innovation to their organizations, resulting in a truly sustainable competitive advantage for that company.

For example, if you are assigned a task that you have no desire to do and cannot find value in, chances are you will be in an operational or tactical mode. You are not deeply invested in the task at hand and simply do what needs to be done to complete it. The task, the work, or the job is simply a means to another end—working for a paycheck so you can do the things you are really passionate about. There is absolutely nothing good or bad or right or wrong with this mode. Alternatively, if you are assigned a task that you cannot wait to dive into and are really excited about, you will more than likely be in your Rudolph space—highly creative and innovative. Again, there is nothing good or bad or right or wrong with any of the four modes. In fact, all are essential to the successful operation of any organization. And if you become completely consumed with your work and are constantly thinking about potential, possibility, and opportunity, you may decide to make the shift to self-employment in the land of entrepreneurship.

It is also important to note that we recognized life/work balance issues at the extreme ends of the percentages spectrum (from 0 to 5 percent and 95 to 100 percent). For example, many entrepreneurs and executives tend to live/breath/eat/sleep/think about their work all of the time. They won't realize it is 3:19 AM because they have been consumed with thoughts about work. In an extreme case, an entrepreneur might spend his or her normal day working and an *additional* eight hours . . . or more . . . working and thinking about work. At the opposite end of the spectrum, not thinking about work at all is generally reflective of someone who may be completely disconnected from his or her job—or organization—altogether and who simply clocks in and clocks out or checks in and checks out. Safety issues could occur as a result of this type of disconnection.

As we have become more familiar with the characteristics of each mode through our research—most specifically, Rudolphs—we have found that each is inspired by different means and appreciates different forms of reward (to be discussed in greater detail in Chapter 8). The beauty of the information presented in Table 3.2 is that it never locks anyone into any specific mode. Whichever mode you are in is dependent upon context, circumstance, and the environment you are in. Consider where you may fit based on the Table in various aspects of your life—at home, at work, with your role in different groups, or your affiliations to various organizations.

Chapter 3 Review

- Employers are typically not aware of their Rudolphs and the latent creative and innovative thinking that comes quite naturally to them.

- Managers who identify and nurture their Rudolphs are leaders in industry.

- Everyone has a degree of *Rudolphness* in them.

- Depending on context and environment, you may be operating in a tactical/operational, facilitative/managerial, creative/innovative, or a visionary/strategic mode.

- All four operational modes are essential to every organization.

NURTURING RUDOLPHS TO MAXIMIZE THEIR INNOVATIVE CONTRIBUTIONS

While Santa's Rudolph looked fairly similar to the other reindeer on the team (with the exception of his glowing nose, of course), Rudolphs in the workplace look just like every other employee, *except* as noted in the last chapter, they think very differently, ask more questions, are inspired by different factors, and typically value a different type of reward. Fortunately, it only takes a conversation or two to recognize Rudolphs who do not seem to fit well within their organization's norms.

We have found that people who behave as mentors in their organization tend to have an uncanny ability to recognize and nurture Rudolphs. They tend to take junior Rudolphs under their wing, give them guidance, and offer an outlet for their creativity. In some cases, it is a direct manager who does this, and in other cases, it might be a senior executive who happens upon a friendly Rudolph and acts to protect him from the harsh realities of most corporate cultures. Mentors may or may not be Rudolphs themselves, but they recognize the potential in Rudolphs and nurture them in an effective and productive way. The short answer to the question, "How do I nurture my Rudolphs?" is to mentor them, take them under your wing, and commit yourself to their success as creative and innovative contributors to your organization. Recognize that they will not always fit in and may need some advocacy and protection to be able to transform their unconventional ideas into reality.

The longer answer to the question of how to nurture Rudolphs involves very specific things you can do (actions, A), once you are aware (A) of your Rudolph's potential, value (V) what Rudolphs bring to the organization, and are thinking (T) about how to leverage their creativity and innovative thinking. Based on the AVTAR model, knowing *what to do* can only be answered once the AVT (awareness, value in awareness, and thinking) has been addressed. Results occur quite naturally within an environment conducive to Rudolphs. The following story demonstrates what it looks like and feels like to value people and nurture their capabilities.

In my opinion, the job of leadership is to inspire and motivate people. Managers severely underestimate their people and their capabilities. Extraordinary performance is not achieved by "managing" people but by "shoulder to shoulder" leadership, treating them as equals in trust and respect. Leaders must transform the mindset from "you versus me" to "us" working together. You can release the power of the minds of the employees, and they will deliver.

I try to lead people by what I would want to see in my leader and with basic coaching skills that you would see in a winning sports team. You have to trust that people have the ability to accomplish their tasks and empower them to make decisions to execute the work. I empower my teams by chartering them to run their part of the business. I challenge them with high goals, am always available for coaching, and often ask teams to talk about their business.

Never come off like the "big honcho." You don't have to remind people that you are the boss, and don't expect to be treated any differently than anyone else. When people leave work, they are homeowners, investors, and coaches in their personal lives. Make them the bosses of their destiny at work. Rally these

(continued)

(continued)
people for success. They will amaze you with their results.

Don Pitcher
Operations Director, C-17 Fuselage, The Boeing Company

From the last chapter, we know that Rudolphs are deeply passionate about their work and truly believe they can and do positively affect change within their organizations. Because they see the world through a lens of potential, possibility, and opportunity—not through rose-colored glasses, but through a true ability to see realistic opportunities and solutions to problems that others cannot see—they want nothing more than to do good work, make their managers and peers look good, and improve their organizations. As a non-Rudolph, it may be difficult to believe, but genuine Rudolphs actually find inspiration in making others look good.

While Rudolphs really shine in their work environments, they tend to have difficulty bringing their ideas to fruition. This is not because of a lack of personal ability but because of an *institutional* or systemic hindrance to action taking. Most managers are not aware of their Rudolphs, and most organizational cultures do not nurture their unique, innovative thinking. In many cases we have seen, the leadership style, organizational culture, and reward structure fail to properly recognize Rudolphs in a manner that inspires them to continue to contribute.

Under such circumstances, a Rudolph's light begins to fade. According to our interviews, in time, Rudolphs purposefully withhold, and ultimately stop sharing ideas with their company leaders—even though the ideas continue to percolate in their minds.

As your organization's cultural revolution begins, your Rudolphs might be difficult to nurture at first—especially because most organizational cultures unwittingly encourage their employees to *check their red noses at the door*. It is a paradox, really. Corporations are spending millions of dollars trying to figure out who their innovative agents of change are—even going so far as to mandate psychological assessments to determine latent creative talent. Today's managers desire—even demand—creative contributions from their employees but are hesitant to accept the inherent risk that comes with innovation.

As discussed in the first chapter, the command-and-control style of management, which is still prevalent today, is antithetical to environments that nurture Rudolphs. Eliciting innovative and creative thinking from employees, in general, requires a transfer of responsibility to them, and most company managers are unwilling to do so. At Boeing C-17, this transfer of responsibility brought about new challenges for their teams. There are over 500 formal (defined as working through the four documented stages of team maturity) teams in the C-17 Program, approximately 3,500 formal teams in the Integrated Defense Systems business unit, and over 4,000 teams at the Boeing enterprise level (meaning, across

The Boeing Company)—all working on *self-initiated* projects. Rather than perpetuating the wedge between their Rudolphs and non-Rudolphs working on the same teams, the roles of leaders and teams had to change. In-house Practitioners in the Employee Involvement (EI) Program created ground rules for working together. Rudolphs and non-Rudolphs on the same team must:

- Meet weekly to identify and manage improvements.
- Commit to projects and a shared vision.
- Develop team-building skills.
- Participate in the learning process.
- Share information and cooperate with one another.

On average, C-17 teams have reported generating $143,000. If you do the math, it does not take long to see the potential. Collectively, those 500+ formal teams have consistently generated savings or revenues in terms of cost-avoidance, cycle-time reduction, new products, and production and process improvements to the tune of millions of dollars each year. Just through the Creative Edge Program, employees and teams have generated savings of over $90 million to their bottom line over the past decade. As impressive as these numbers are, do not be tempted to identify your Rudolphs and throw them into teams and expect the same results. The secret is to nurture your Rudolphs, which will inspire them to do great things and generate high-level business results on their own on an ongoing basis. Remember, the elements that you cannot see are the ones that generate organizational greatness.

If the nurturing element is missing, the paradox of management wanting creativity and innovation without the ability to transfer responsibility to the workers causes Rudolphs to learn to intentionally stay under the radar. It amazed us to discover how many Rudolphs out there are purposefully withholding cost-saving or revenue-generating ideas. Management's inability to transfer responsibility to employees significantly decreases the effectiveness of teams. The nurturing element has been all but nonexistent for many Rudolphs, so they tend to operate from a set of survival skills. These skills are a result of conditioning from being sidelined or sabotaged by peers or their direct managers. Rudolphs want to succeed, but more importantly, they want their organizations and the people around them to succeed. They live by values rather than rules, and sometimes make career-limiting moves (what we refer to as "CLMs") when at odds with the dominant or prevailing culture of their company. Because they tend to ask the tough questions that others are afraid or unwilling to ask, it can appear as if they are intending to rock the boat. This is simply not the case. Sometimes Rudolphs save the day, and other times they have to jump ship, or worse, are thrown overboard.

As previously noted, Rudolphs look at their organizations through a lens of potential, possibility, and opportunity, although the traditional corporate culture requires and rewards conformity, compromise, and control. In this scenario, it is like doing the tango on a high wire. The simple act of nurturing your Rudolphs will bring them their highest level of satisfaction—effecting sustainable change and seeing their ideas in action. We refer to this highest level of satisfaction as leaving an indelible *hoofprint* on their organization. The irony is that companies are literally begging for radical creativity and innovation, and most are unaware of the fountain of creativity right under their own (brown) noses.

A SMALL BUT MIGHTY HERD

We believe every organization has a small but mighty herd of Rudolphs just waiting for an opportunity to shine. From large, global corporations to small, family owned businesses—whether it is a private, public, or not-for-profit organization—Rudolphs are sprinkled throughout every company and hold positions on every rung of the corporate ladder, from CEO to frontline worker. While some may be heroic leaders of innovation, others are quiet but deeply committed agents of change, not only seeing opportunities to act but also taking action. You might be wondering why Rudolphs would continue to work for a company where they do not fit in and where they feel they have to temper their involuntary but highly, innovative thinking. We discovered that their unique ability to see possibility and potential opportunities around every corner—along with their capacity to make a positive difference—keeps many Rudolphs from seeking greener pastures, unless the culture becomes too difficult, painful, or toxic for them to stay.

Rudolphs tend to be a bit isolated (typically, by their own choice) and generally save their energy for creative outlets *outside* of work. Over time, they might stumble on a handful of other Rudolphs within their organization, but even then, the existence of this small herd is relatively unnoticed. Rudolphs do an excellent job of nurturing each other and leveraging each other's talents, titles, and political influence to get things accomplished. All the while, most employers have no idea that they have a full herd of Rudolphs in the stable. Ironically, it is becoming rather commonplace for corporations to seek creativity and innovation from expensive, outside sources by acquiring new talent. Another prevalent and expensive practice is for larger companies to acquire smaller, more nimble and creative companies. Ironically, the larger, more dominant culture tends to squish the acquired group's creative juices in a formal, strategic merging of diametrical cultures. Even though we have seen and read about it time and time again, it continues to be a common practice among behemoth companies.

THREE STEPS TO NURTURING YOUR RUDOLPHS

If you think you might have some Rudolphs in your herd, there are three things you can do right away to start the process of getting them back on the radar screen, and the easiest is to have them read this book. It demonstrates that you are aware that Rudolphs think differently than their cohorts, and it will help them see they are not alone in being different from their peers. The process of getting them back on the radar screen will be as easy as opening your mind (and ears) to what your Rudolphs share with you. Chances are that your Rudolphs will have *a lot* to say once they are given the chance, after first being convinced that there will be no repercussions for sharing their thoughts.

Step 1: Open Your Mind

The first step you have to take is to open your mind to a different way of thinking. In doing so, you create an environment in which it is safe to voice ideas. Depending on how healthy or unhealthy your organization's culture is, you may need to do some foundation-building work before you are in a position to identify and nurture your Rudolphs. We share tools on how to build a supportive team-based culture as well as ideas for leadership style in Chapter 5 and appropriate reward structures in Chapters 6 through 8. Rudolphs will not allow themselves to be drawn out of the herd if they perceive it is not safe. Remember, many of their past efforts have made them a proverbial target, so expect them to be a little shy at revealing their red noses under the mud.

Also remember that these people have had nonstop thoughts about how to improve their work environment, solve a nagging problem, and improve performance for a very long time. In fact, we have met many Rudolphs who did not share their creativity and innovations for decades! Consider the millions of dollars of cost savings that were not realized prior to Boeing C-17's cultural revolution. If you happen to be the manager of a Rudolph or two, be prepared to take a lot of notes because what they share may be overwhelming. If you have been asking for a fountain of creativity from your people, you are going to get it via a fire hose when you unleash the voices of your Rudolphs. Be prepared with an open mind, and have a process in place to be able to move on ideas that might have merit (ideas with legs).

Step 2: Identify Unique Unmet Needs of Your Rudolphs

While the first thing you can do is open your mind to what your Rudolphs are going to share, the second step is to identify what their specific needs are. Almost every Rudolph we have come into contact with has needs that are unique to their counterparts. Here are some examples of needs that Boeing Rudolphs shared with us:

- Rudolphs need an outlet to share ideas on a *regular* basis.
- Most Rudolphs need protection from their direct manager because Rudolphs are commonly perceived as a threat—unless that manager is savvy at

69

realizing the value Rudolphs bring to the organization.

- Rudolphs' thinking is best leveraged when they know it is okay to take risks. Rudolphs' ideas generally do not come nicely packaged. They tend to be unconventional ideas and sometimes require unconventional means to effectively implement. You will need to be okay with unconventional thinking—particularly if you are not an unconventional thinker. This does not entail agreeing to whatever ideas your Rudolphs have. If you do not understand where the thinking came from or how it is going to work, ask lots of questions. Chances are, when your Rudolphs share their thought process used in getting to the ideas, everything will make more sense. As their manager, you will be able to provide more information about the constraints that Rudolphs may not be privy to.

- Many Rudolphs need to be protected from ill-willed peers who may not appreciate or value the dynamic that Rudolphs can and do bring to the organization.

- All Rudolphs need other people to be successful, and they value collaboration immensely. You will need to provide team training to facilitate the process of building teams in which Rudolphs work with non-Rudolphs. This is detailed further in Chapter 5.

- Rudolphs need the ability to execute their ideas, but not in a haphazard fashion. You need to create a system for capturing, funneling, reviewing, modifying (if necessary), and implementing ideas, which is also detailed in Chapter 5.

Step 3: Put Processes in Place that Encourage Implementation

In nurturing Rudolphs—as opposed to non-Rudolphs—the two most important tools they are given include a voice (empowerment) and the ability to implement the ideas that improve organizational conditions. Through many interviews with Boeing C-17 personnel as well as Rudolphs at other organizations, we have found that the greatest limiting factor for Rudolphs in contributing their creativity and innovations tends to be their direct or middle managers. Because of the system midlevel managers work in, they tend to face a different kind of pressure than the workers or executive staff. Their population tends to be pulled in the most different—and sometimes diametrical—directions. Rather than leveraging the creative ideas from their Rudolphs, they may tend to micromanage or sometimes even take credit for the ideas, which quickly dims the lit noses of Rudolphs.

In the lessons-learned phase of Boeing C-17's cultural revolution, the executive staff recognized that the system their culture operated in discouraged midlevel managers from moving quickly on change initiatives. These days, when a proposed change of some sort is necessary, it still comes from the top, but it bypasses the traditional hierarchical ladder and goes straight to the floor—to the people actually doing the work. Then the top and bottom put *the squeeze* on the midlevel managers. With pressure from both ends, midlevel managers have no choice but to acquiesce. While this sounds rather imposing, it is actually a relief to midlevel managers because the responsibility for success or failure does not fall on their shoulders alone. Executives and workers share in the responsibility for success or failure with midlevel managers. This sharing of responsibility eliminates most of the finger pointing faced in organizations and encourages alignment of the proposed change to long-term strategies.

An excellent example of communication from senior leadership going directly to the workers can be seen in a recent e-mail from Vice President/General Manager Global Mobility Systems, Jean Chamberlin. It not only inspires collaborative efforts during challenging times, but it also addresses recognition of success stories. The language used is very reflective of a people-centric culture.

GMS Teammates,

Last week I informed managers across Global Mobility Systems [GMS] about some of the cost-cutting measures we have to take as Boeing maneuvers through some challenging economic times. Our goal across GMS, Integrated Defense Systems and Boeing is to find ways to reduce costs while maintaining our strengths and improving our productivity.

For the C-17 Program, we certainly must find ways to meet and/or exceed the expectations of our domestic and international customers. Only by keeping the C-17 an affordable solution can we sustain existing customers and gain new ones, ensuring a long future in Long Beach.

I am welcoming all of you to provide whatever suggestions you may have on how we can drive our costs down while maintaining the GMS brand of quality that makes us the world leader in mobility products. Some of the areas in which we already are taking steps include reducing travel whenever possible and getting a handle on electronic devices by making sure they are dispersed efficiently. Your manager can inform you about other efforts.

We all need to work together and challenge ourselves to find ways to be more productive. And let us know your success stories as well as ways your team has helped make our operations more cost effective and productive. Please respond to this e-mail with success stories and any and all suggestions to further reduce costs.

Together we can get through these tough times.

Jean

Jean Chamberlin
Vice President/General Manager, Global Mobility Systems, Integrated Defense Systems, The Boeing Company

Please recognize that if the culture had not been revolutionized, this letter would most likely have ended up ignored, or worse, scoffed at by employees. But because Boeing C-17 has done the work—addressed their thinking, revisited what leadership means to them, developed a solid institutional memory (or Corporate Constitution), and continues to encourage and nurture their Rudolph Culture—this letter had significant meaning to all employees. Referring to our AVTAR model, Chamberlin provides the awareness (A) and offers a sense of value (V) to working together to make it through the current state of the global economy. Because responsibility and ownership of the culture has been shifted to the employees, they will very likely embrace her request and be inspired to think (T) of things they can do (action, A) to get the desired results (R), which include cost-cutting practices without compromising quality by finding ways to be more effective and productive. As a result of Chamberlin's e-mail, 50 to 70 ideas worthy of consideration were generated immediately. Given our experiences with Boeing C-17's people over the past few years, we have no doubt that more ideas are brewing and new success stories are being captured. The following story from a C-17 wing tank mechanic illustrates this shift of responsibility felt by employees.

I am a wing tank mechanic. We no longer leave our brains and common sense at the gate. Our leadership encourages us to think out of the box to improve our business and remove the barriers. We see our cost and performance numbers, and we are saving the company money. The mechanics are listening to each other, sharing knowledge and information. Because of the transformation, we feel like part of the company.

Jake B. Hampton, Jr.
Wing IPT 5S focal, Wing Tank Mechanic C-17, The Boeing Company

OUR CHALLENGE TO YOU

Consider who might be a Rudolph in your organization, take an interest in understanding how they think, and commit yourself to joint success. Know that they are committed to yours. Also consider the four modes of operation: tactical or operational, facilitative or managerial, creative or innovative, and visionary or strategic. As you become more aware of what mode the people around you are operating in, you will be able to address the psychology of change (AVTAR) for each mode. There are distinct forms of recognition, rewards, and motivators that address each mode (to be discussed in detail in Chapter 8), and knowing this allows you to be more effective with all types of people. Rudolphs are revolutionaries—drivers of change—and businesses reap the rewards of extraordinary results when they nurture and create an environment that supports and encourages innovative thought and creative contributions from Rudolphs.

Chapter 4 Review

- Consider whether your Rudolphs are *checking their red noses at the door.*

- Rudolph Cultures are based on values rather than rules.

- Every organization, large and small, has a small but mighty herd of Rudolphs.

- Open your mind, identify unmet needs, and have processes in place to nurture creative and innovative thinking from Rudolphs and non-Rudolphs.

- When responsibility and ownership has been shifted to employees, organizational greatness is a distinct possibility.

ESTABLISHING A TEAM-BASED RUDOLPH CULTURE

It is important to note that we define culture as the manifestation of every exchange and interaction every day between every person (including workers, managers, executives, suppliers, and customers) affiliated with an organization. An organization's culture is not just the responsibility of management, it belongs to everyone. It is no wonder that cultural change can be difficult, but as shown in this book, it can occur on a grand scale in a relatively short period of time (10,000 people over a six-year period in one of the most regulated and bureaucratic industries).

We believe there are four elements that, when integrated, make up what we refer to as the *Four Pillars of Organizational Greatness*. Chapters 5 through 8 address each pillar individually, including establishing a Rudolph Culture, redefining leadership, developing a Corporate Constitution, and creating an Alternative and Aligned Reward Structure. Recognize that organizational greatness is not dependent on how strong each pillar is individually. Greatness is dependent on how well the four pillars hold up the structure—in other words, how well each pillar is integrated with the other three.

We begin with establishing a Rudolph Culture in response to the problems noted in Chapter One faced by companies with regard to eliciting innovative thinking and employee engagement. Many managers react to this ambivalence and lack of engagement by mandating process improvement or performance management initiatives. Even worse, some management teams tie these typically poorly planned strategies to workers' performance reviews without addressing how the strategies affect each individual's work. Rather than taking the time to consider which strategies, tools, and initiatives are best suited for the organization's long-term vision, management makes the workers responsible for the success of the initiatives and strategies. Before long, a flavor-of-the-month culture is born, only fueling the perpetuation of the disengaged and/or dysfunctional corporate culture. Almost every large organization we have worked with has experienced this type of culture at some point in its journey . . . and many have never gotten beyond it. The cycle of forcing employees to contribute or be engaged in carrying out the mandates—by tying the reward structure to employee performance—only further diminishes any possibility for building a high-performing, team-based Rudolph Culture.

In addition to internal behaviors, we believe an organization's culture is also influenced by how senior leadership and management respond to external circumstances. In many cases, management either reacts hastily without consideration for the internal dynamics, or they resist letting go of what has historically constituted their competitive advantage. For the past century, first to market or faster/smaller/cheaper to produce has been considered strong criteria for generating a competitive advantage. In the past 20 years, new or expanded services, improved quality, and lower price via cost-cutting process improvement initiatives have been targeted goals to generate a competitive advantage. In today's expansive global market riddled with the current global financial crises, vast improvements in transportation, communication, and tracking technologies, as well as leaps in computing capabilities (those things we have traditionally considered to be sustainable competitive advantages) are all now replicable in a fairly short period of time by domestic, international, and even virtual companies (those that operate without brick-and-mortar facilities from all over the world).

As you might have guessed, we believe the only *sustainable* competitive advantages over a long period of time are nontangibles, including, but not limited to, the individual and collective knowledge base of workers, leadership style, an innovative culture, and creating an "experience" for customers (rather than simply a transaction between company and customer). In the simplest of terms, the nontangibles are reflected in the "people part" of an organization and can be frightening to management because nontangibles can be very difficult to properly assess, measure, and control. In the world of people-centric organizations, *one size does not fit all*, which throws a complete monkey wrench in the realm of process improvement, problem solving, performance management, and generating innovations. However, organizations like Boeing's C-17 Program that value their nontangibles (primarily their people) are winning the race to secure an enormous sustainable competitive advantage. During interviews with two of the Employee Involvement (EI) Practitioners, Richard Nicholson and Charles Macias thoughtfully explained that EI is at the epicenter of B-O-*EI*-N-G and that their Rudolphs were the people who started the revolution that transformed the Boeing C-17 Program into a world-class leader. On average, every employee we interviewed had been with Boeing (or previously, McDonnell Douglas) for over 20 years. Employee involvement and engagement is at the very core of all people-centric organizations.

ELICITING ONGOING CREATIVE AND INNOVATIVE INPUT

Once you are able to identify and nurture your bright lights, the next step is to build a system to generate ongoing creative and innovative employee engagement and contribution. The development of a Rudolph Culture will ensure proper encouragement and support so that it can become a sustainable competitive advantage regardless of industry or size of organization. As previously mentioned, within the Boeing C-17 Program, this sustainable competitive advantage has impacted the bottom line by over $90 million during a 10-year time frame and continues to generate greater savings every year. Between the Creative Edge Program and Team-Based Business Improvement (TBBI) Programs, savings and generated revenues equaled hundreds of millions of dollars. According to metrics that have been collected over the past several years, we are pleased to report that there is a direct correlation between Boeing C-17's employee cost reduction incentive programs and employee satisfaction levels, which have continued to stay high. The employee satisfaction levels are at the "Premier Company" level. Based on our findings, happy Boeing workers are creative and innovative Boeing workers! The following story depicts how applying concepts and practices to engage employees not only transformed the dominant engineering culture, but also increased employee satisfaction in the process.

Applying principles of Employee Involvement (EI) and Employee Engagement (EE) has helped our engineering organization transform to a high-performance team-based culture. As an engineering center of excellence
(*continued*)

(*continued*)

and a high-performance organization, we have been able to develop, design, test, build, and deliver our world-class products to our government and other global customers. We have accomplished our goals and deliverables by leveraging principles of EI and Lean in everything we do.

Based on our shared vision of 100 percent implementation and institutionalization of team-based culture, we have been able to promote and integrate innovation, productivity, employee satisfaction, and diversity. Such EI components have collectively helped us achieve business results and globally increase our competitiveness, while adding value to our shareholders' interest.

Kami Moghaddam, EdD
Engineering Integration EI & Lean+ Leader, The Boeing Company

In establishing a Rudolph Culture, the most critical element to consider is ensuring Rudolphs and non-Rudolphs have a safe environment to share and execute ideas. As a manager (whether you are a Rudolph or not), you must recognize that perceptions are as powerful as reality. In fact, we believe they are one and the same. Therefore, you might believe that you have created a safe environment in which contributions can be made, but your employees do not appear to be engaged in the process. This is a management moment—meaning, it is now your responsibility to find out what is missing. In many cases, we have found that managers, who are able to truly recognize the value of employee engagement and shift their thinking as a result, have had to reintroduce themselves to their workers. This shift in thinking changes how they manage and interact with the people around them. There are often trust issues that need to be addressed during the process of establishing a Rudolph Culture. Our advice is to be patient and continue to commit to the success of people around you. It may take time, and people typically test the water before the process is running smoothly.

Because most organization cultures are influenced by 90 percent non-Rudolphs, we will also give you tools to help you manage and foster creative and innovative thinking from your non-Rudolphs. The idea is *not* to create a separation between Rudolphs and non-Rudolphs—we already have that in most organizations. The goal is to nurture relationships between the two so that all four modes—tactical (i.e., workers), facilitative (managers), creative (Rudolphs), and strategic (executives)—work together to be as effective as possible.

Taking the concepts we have shared from identifying and nurturing individual Rudolphs to building a Rudolph Culture requires identifying the thinking behind the building process. It would be of no service to you to simply share the initiatives Boeing C-17 uses because there would be no foundation for you to build on. Boeing C-17's cultural revolution grew out of trial and error and some pivotal ah-ha moments by leadership. Because we have captured their process, we can now replicate the thinking with intentional design. Your process of transformation might look different than theirs. This is okay. In fact, we would hope that yours will be unique, unless you are the same size as the Boeing C-17 Program, are manufacturing the same product, with the same customer, and in the same industry ... you get the point.

The "Ten Lessons Learned on the Journey" that were shared with us from the leadership of Boeing's C-17 Program, reflect the thinking behind the tools used, initiatives introduced, and decisions made. These lessons continue to significantly influence the culture at Boeing C-17 today and are transferable to any size and type of organization. The only requirement is that *everyone within the organization must share a common purpose.*

Ten Lessons Learned on the Boeing C-17 Journey

1. The law of change: If you always do what you have always done, you will get what you have always gotten!

2. Change is hard for people if they do not know where they are going or why.

3. It is a *journey*, not an event—we are still on our way.

4. Leadership must execute business strategies through others. When employees are part of defining what it means to them, there is more personal commitment.

5. Leadership must be persistent; stay the course and refuse to give up.

6. All training must include immediate application to the team.

7. You must have a written plan.

8. Recognition must be part of the process.

9. Traditional roles must change (leadership and team members).

10. Enjoy the journey!

We are going to discuss lessons one, two, three, and six in this chapter regarding establishing a Rudolph Culture. Lessons four, five, and nine will be addressed in Chapter 6, "Redefining Leadership." Lessons seven and nine (again) will be addressed in Chapter 7, "Developing a Corporate Constitution." Lesson eight will be addressed in Chapter 8, "Creating an Alternative and Aligned Reward Structure," and Lesson Ten—*Enjoy the Journey!*—will be shared in the Epilogue.

LESSON ONE: DOING WHAT YOU'VE ALWAYS DONE

The first lesson, *doing what you've always done will get you what you've always gotten,* came out of the senior leaders' awareness that companies tend to be slow on action. The value of this awareness is if you want a different outcome, you must change the process, the product, or both, NOW! This influenced management's thinking about their technical-social system within the Boeing C-17 Program. Historically, and as with most companies, the technical aspects of the business far outweigh the sociocultural elements. The technical aspects include the processes, procedures, goals, technology, financial resources, equipment/tooling/electronics, and other mechanical features and comprise approximately 10 percent of the formal and informal aspects of organizational life. The other 90 percent, the sociocultural elements, include personal beliefs, personal assumptions, perceptions, attitudes, feelings of anger or pride, personal values, personal interactions, and team norms.[*]

In establishing a team-based Rudolph Culture, having created a formalized EI Program balances the technical/sociocultural scale through commitment and engagement. Assessment is an effective tool that is most useful for addressing the technical and sociocultural balance. There are literally hundreds of types of organizational assessment tools available, but two primary ones used in Boeing C-17's journey included a SWOT analysis (examining the organization's *S*trengths, *W*eaknesses, *O*pportunities, and *T*hreats) as connected to the Program's Vision, and a set of six simple questions that were used to facilitate the

---

[*] Information regarding the 90/10 split comes from the *E.I. Toolkit for Growth and Productivity* Presentation—created by E.I. Practitioners, Dr. Charles Macias, Dr. Richard Nicholson, and other EI Team Members.

process of taking an honest look at where your organization is by the way it values people. Sometimes it can be difficult for management to take an objective look at the organization because we tend to be more invested in what we believe exists than what truly exists. The six questions Boeing management used to take an honest assessment of their current state of affairs involving people included:

1. Does everyone in the organization understand our customers and their business?

2. Do leadership and management have a clear vision?

3. Does the vision include language about people and teamwork?

4. Do the employees know what the vision is?

5. Has leadership and management created strategies and supporting objectives at all levels of the organization? Are they aligned with each other?

6. Are all employees encouraged to be involved in decision making and improvements for their part of the business?

Question number six is critical—employees must be involved at the decision-making level. To do so, they must be trained in creating budgets, meeting management, conflict resolution, as well as other business functions that are typically facilitated or led by management, rather than frontline workers. As we previously noted, responsibility and ownership must be transferred over to the people doing the work. You can easily see how stifling it would be if management were trying to encourage employee involvement and engagement but did not offer tools or information that would allow employees to really *own* their part of the business. You simply cannot have one without the other. Engagement at the level that will drive innovation into your business requires a transfer of responsibility to the workers.

LESSON TWO: CHANGE IS HARD FOR PEOPLE IF THEY DON'T KNOW WHERE THEY'RE GOING OR WHY

The second lesson, *change is hard for people if they don't know where they're going or why*, requires leaders and managers to share the vision often so that everyone can see it. Many companies share their organizational vision, but it has no emotional value to employees. We believe people do not *naturally* resist change. Naturally resisting change implies that *all* change would be resisted, and we know this is not true. For example, if employees were told that management was going to double bonuses at the end of the quarter, we do not believe there would be much resistance expressed! Resistance comes from the inability to know how a proposed change is going to impact employees at a personal level. Resistance is also apparent when employees do not have *insider* information that lets them know why the proposed change is necessary. Within the Boeing C-17 Program, the executive leadership realized that imposing change might work for the short term, but to get the level of engagement they were asking for, *employees* would have to be the change agents.

LESSON THREE: IT IS A JOURNEY

The third lesson, *it's a journey, not an event*, addresses one of today's most prevalent and crippling thought paradigms. Our larger, societal culture has become fixated on short-term metrics. This has infiltrated most organizations, with some even going so far as posting daily stock prices where employees can watch them go up and down every day. Management's thinking behind this practice is that employees will work harder when the stock price decreases. Employees, on the other hand, recognize all too quickly, that their individual efforts have no direct effect on whether the stock price goes up or down. They can work as hard as they have ever worked, and the stock price can and does go down. Think of the message this practice sends to employees.

Boeing C-17's leadership had another ah-ha moment when they realized the value of not stopping one effort and starting a new one; instead, they built efforts into the journey. This thinking has several implications, but the one we would like you to most consider is to introduce only those initiatives that fit into the larger strategy and vision. It is never the initiative that fails. Most often, we see initiatives introduced without consideration of how other parts of the organization will be affected. Once you recognize that the organization is a dynamic, connected system that is part of a larger system, you will use more discretion in deciding what tools and initiatives are implemented. However, if the mindset continues to be "if this one doesn't work, we'll try another and another … "; eventually, no one takes any initiative seriously, even if it is actually the most appropriate one to implement.

This is one area where you can really leverage the thinking of your Rudolphs because they are generally the people asking, "Why are we doing this?" While it may appear that Rudolphs' questioning is indicative of resistance, know that it is not. Rudolphs naturally see their environment as a system, recognizing the connections between elements within and beyond the organization and having the ability to clearly separate *symptoms* of problems from *causes* of problems. It is simply how their mind works. Your Rudolphs' questioning ensures that the tools and initiatives introduced to your organization have gone through a rigorous, thought-filled process.

LESSON SIX: ALL TRAINING MUST INCLUDE IMMEDIATE APPLICATION TO THE TEAM

The sixth lesson is *all training must include immediate application to the team*. The greatest power found in training is actually in the *discussion by the team members regarding how it immediately affects each one of their jobs.* This discussion is as critical as the training itself. We have all experienced training or have learned new concepts at conferences that sound great, but that is the extent of it. The missing link is how the training affects me right now. If organizations spent half of their training resources on facilitating the discussion around training, employees would likely need half the training! For any type of training to be effective, managers, trainers, and facilitators need to use the AVTAR model.

In using AVTAR, the person conducting the training sets the stage for raising awareness (A) about the training. The manager is also responsible for presenting com-pelling reasons so employees can find value (V) in their new awareness (compelling to the employees, not just the trainer or manager). After employees recognize the value of the training, their thinking (T) is influenced, and they are more able to choose actions (A) that will lead to the desired results (R). Without this simple process, it is likely that managers would simply tell employees what to do and hope for the desired results to occur. We never conduct workshops or classes without first confirming the benefits of the curriculum to the client. There is no sense in jumping into training unless they can connect the value of it to their immediate work. With-out application, training is simply a waste of efforts and resources.

Ensuring training has immediate application to employees requires a simple facilitative conversation with very few rules of engagement. First, every team member must be present at the time of the conversation—present in person or on a conference call. This is not effective to conduct via e-mail. All team members must be given an opportunity to share how they see the initiative affecting their job *as if the initiative were already in place*. For example, one of the C-17 team empowerment areas is Financial Management. Teams of employees can be empowered to monitor and manage their own budgets, so they have to be trained on some financial management concepts. In this case, learning financial management concepts teaches employees how to design a budget and facilitates the process of discussing the budget with information, rather than instinct. It also teaches employees how to find the right information and keep track of costs. In the end, it teaches employees how to take responsibility for staying within the budget they themselves created, which eliminates—and at the very least minimizes—finger pointing at management for not giving the team enough resources. Success and failure becomes the responsibility of the team, rather than just the manager.

Team training and learning are essential and valued elements of Boeing C-17's Rudolph Culture. If your work entails designing training, know that it must be relevant to people's current work as well as to the larger organizational values and vision. The Boeing C-17 EI area has a highly developed team-training program involving knowledge transfer *and* application of the knowledge. As the EI Leadership shared with us, "Let the team training begin, and watch the 'magic' happen with application." The days of training for the sake of checking a box are over. It is archaic, costly, and a serious demotivator for employees.

Because of the high number of Rudolphs and non-Rudolphs working together on teams, the C-17's EI in-house practitioners spend a significant amount of time teaching employees how to be effective members of highly empowered and self-directed teams. If workers have come from another organization that did not have a Rudolph Culture, the AVTAR model is even more important because ingrained filters and conditioning may stifle a new employee's ability to see beyond actions and results. Before application—or actions—can be taken, the awareness, value, and thinking must be addressed.

Some of the training required for all Boeing C-17 teams includes:

- Developing a case for change
- Developing a team charter
- Facilitating effective meetings
- Brainstorming techniques
- Decision-making methodologies
- Empowerment
- Feedback
- Group dynamics

- Problem solving
- Strategic planning
- Team formation
- Communication and team conflict
- Leadership development
- Coaching

Again, this is not management training conducted for managers only. This training is team training for the people doing the work on the shop floor, in the office, manufacturers, engineers, managers ... everyone.

THE CREATIVE EDGE PROGRAM

Another important element of leveraging your Rudolph Factor revolves around how the culture is structured. The Boeing C-17 Program management thoughtfully altered its highly layered and bureaucratic structure to allow for a higher level of lateral and interrelational communication. This alternative approach is not radical, nor does it require prohibitive time or resource commitments. It offers a structured and sustainable process for contributing innovations. Within their Rudolph Culture, Boeing has a formalized Employee Cost Reduction Incentive Program. And believe us when we say, "This is not your father's employee suggestion program!"

At the most fundamental level, The Boeing Company is aware of and recognizes the value in eliciting creative and innovative thinking from employees (the A through V of AVTAR). As a result, management's thinking began to shift from *imposing* creativity and innovation *upon* its employees to *drawing* it *from* employees. Even though employees desire to have a voice and a process to share their ideas, most employee suggestion programs are short-lived for a variety of reasons. In some cases, the process of accepting and processing ideas was not well thought out, and the review process becomes a tremendous bottleneck for any innovation. Other times, the suggestion program is simply lip service—employees give ideas but never get feedback or see them manifested into reality. It does not take long for employees to recognize that their thinking and suggestions are not valued. Once this occurs, it is a difficult and time-consuming process to reverse.

At the heart of eliciting creative and innovative thinking from Boeing C-17 employees are the Creative Edge and Team-Based Business Improvements (TBBI) Programs. These are both vital elements to leveraging Boeing's Rudolph Factor and have resulted in a cost savings of over $90 million over the past 10 years. The objective of the Creative Edge Program is to make the product (the Boeing C-17 cargo aircraft) more affordable by soliciting, evaluating, facilitating, and rewarding cost-saving ideas submitted by employees. It is an integral part of the EI Reward and Recognition system. Every year, hundreds of employees contribute their innovative ideas and are awarded from $50 to $250 per employee plus 1 to 2 percent of the first year net savings (FYNS) if applicable. We believe the largest amount of money paid to an employee was $32,000. The following story is from a Creative Edge participant and shows how having a mechanism and process to capture creative and innovative ideas can result in employees feeling greater ownership of the success of the overall organization.

> Through the Creative Edge Program, every employee is encouraged and empowered to continuously make significant improvements to quality, safety, cost, and processes in the production of the C-17 airlifter—achieving the true spirit of Employee Involvement with pride of ownership. There is no better feeling or motivation in knowing that, yes, I can make a difference.
>
> Wayne C. Coleman
> Creative Edge Participant and Team Lead, C-17 Final Function, The Boeing Company

The beauty of the Creative Edge Program is that it is available to and accessible by any employee who has an innovative idea. From our interviews, we learned that not everyone participates, but every person expressed a sense of value in having a process that captures a great idea if one comes to mind. By their very nature, Rudolphs tend to be the primary users of the Creative Edge Program.

There is a small percentage of employees that tend to generate new ideas and test their feasibility through the Creative Edge Program on a continual basis—the regulars. Because this is a voluntary program, it is not taking away from getting normal job functions completed. However, anytime you have employees who work closely with a process and/or product, ideas for improvement are bound to occur. In a Rudolph Culture, employees take ownership of their work and of the organization's success by suggesting improvements, solving problems, and presenting innovative ideas to the Review Team.

The Review Team includes a cross-functional team of highly skilled and qualified individuals from all facets of the C-17 Program. The Creative Edge Program is supported by subject matter experts (SME) within their responsible areas. Each supporting Executive Leader has appointed a team member to represent his or her organization on the Review Team. The members include managers and senior managers ranging from Production to all other facets of support functions including Supplier Management, Manufacturing Estimating, as well as the Quality and Affordability Areas. Review Team members are responsible for meeting twice a month to review and approve suggestions and recommend those with potential to higher levels of review. To date, over 1,000 suggestions have been evaluated and reviewed. The following story depicts how the Creative Edge Program was transformed from a nonfunctioning program to a "Best Practice" within the aerospace industry.

During my 20-year career, I have had the honor of developing and implementing several improvements. As we know, some accomplished projects can bring a sense of pride while others constitute a "check off the box" routine. The project I chose was one of the biggest in my work and is still very exciting to me.

The assignment began as a problem. No one wanted anything to do with it because it had repeatedly failed in the past. This project involved cost reductions and employee suggestions with tiered rewards. It was called the Creative Edge Program. It had a long history of losing money on paid awards, and in addition, ideas were not being implemented. They had lost millions of dollars, and the program's name alone had such a negative association that it caused people to just leave the room while they grumbled silently. Employees refused to use it. Needless to say, the company needed this type of program—if anyone could figure out how to make it work. It seemed there were details missing that could be causing the continued failures. Everyone I knew who had been assigned to manage this program took what was given to them and wanted to make it work without changing much of anything. The failures continued, and the numbers of discouraged people mounted.

I was given the challenge to make this program work, and my approach was immediately different. I took what was given to me and did some research on

why the program had failed so miserably. My director, Ed Schaniel, along with every executive leader, vice president, and general manager of the C-17 Program thereafter were always big supporters and very instrumental with empowerment to make the necessary changes and open doors for what was to happen next. I identified who made it fail, what caused it to fail, and why it failed. Once I completed the first part of my research, I briefed the necessary team of executives on the findings. After they heard the details of my review, they were eager to help. I requested that each director appoint a subject matter expert from their organization to represent them at a two-day offsite and to represent them as a monthly member on a review board. On the first day of the offsite with this team of experts, I made a recommendation saying, "Each of you is here today to share what you can to build a completely new cost reduction program." I added, "You are the experts. I am throwing out the old guideline that has never worked and am replacing it with a new process flow and procedure that we as a team will design." The team seemed surprised that this had never before been done, and calmness filled the room. The tension diminished, and the team seemed really excited to move forward with this plan. The Creative Edge Review Team worked diligently toward a common goal to redesign a program of the future and to apply a new business plan that
(*continued*)

(*continued*)

amazed all of the executive leadership. It took longer than the two days to tie up several loose ends, though at the end a tremendous effort provided great business results.

It has now been over 10 years, and the program is still functioning beautifully. The employees participate in the program, and they are highly involved in the idea implementation from its inception to its completion. The platform is set to ensure full buy-in from all executive stakeholders. The review board now consists of 23 appointed subject matter experts who help vote and implement new cost reduction and safety ideas. Today, through this program, I have been able to document over a whopping $90 million in cost reduction. It works! The Creative Edge Program's success has also been recognized as a "Best Practice" within the aerospace industry and was acknowledged during our Baldrige Award presentation in 1998. It is also captured through our Lean Manufacturing Assessments, 2005–2008, as a Best Practice.

My first thought was "Wow!" How much better can I describe the joy that comes from taking a difficult task and being able to make it work better than ever expected? This accomplishment meant so much to me because I was really terrified of the assignment, yet I really wanted to try something different to explore the possibilities of potential success. The thought of getting the same results as before disturbed me, yet the opportunity to be able to report something different and better was also a possibility. I believe this means that when something doesn't seem right, I can take a different perspective. I can look at it from a different angle and allow myself to think differently from those before me. I need to know that sometimes the information that lies in the dark can be the key to the things that can be seen during the day. Just being able to make this program work effectively with my team was a great victory for me and for the C-17 Program at The Boeing Company. I loved it!

Rosie Robles-Gleason,
Creative Edge Project Manager, The Boeing Company

Because the culture seeks greater benefits for everyone, there is a constant evaluating, reenergizing, and re-creating of the incentive-based programs. In fact, there is a team currently researching the benefits to employees by awarding points rather than cash. Other reward programs use points (one point = one dollar) where employees can choose to spend their points in a variety of ways. By design, the Creative Edge Program is a win-win for everyone involved. Boeing receives creative and innovation improvements and solutions on an ongoing basis, and if viable, the employee who submitted the idea (or the team) receives a small percentage of the first year net savings (FYNS). There are four Creative Edge Levels (as seen in Table 5.1).

Table 5.1 Creative Edge Program Structure

Level	Employee Receives	Description	Maximum Per Team
1	$50	Suggestion is accepted, validated, and reviewed for possible higher levels. It has the potential to save a minimum of $5,000.	$500
2	$250	Suggestion must be implemented and have potential to save $5,000 to $24,999.	$2,500
3	1% to 2% First Year Net Sales	Suggestion must be implemented and reviewed by Estimating, Industrial, and Affordability. It must save or reduce $25,000 or more for the first year after implementation (not cost avoidance).	First Year Net Sales based on MD-7091 (Boeing policy number)
4	$50	Must be a valid safety suggestion. No cost reduction minimum is necessary. Only Foreign Object Debris (FOD) and Safety along with approval and the idea must be implemented.	$500

RELATIONSHIP BY OBJECTIVES

Another program used to fully engage employees in their work and the Boeing Vision is the Relationship by Objectives (RBO) Program. This program, which is made up of employees, is intended to facilitate union and nonunion employees working together to achieve objectives that affect everyone. The program uses employee-generated information to focus on initiatives that create and maintain an attractive, secure, and safe workplace. Unfortunately in most traditional organizations, a significant percentage of workers experience quality-of-work-life issues that negatively effect their contribution to the organization. This particular RBO forum supports a team-based Rudolph Culture by providing a favorable setting for employees to meet and resolve issues that are having a real or perceived negative effect on their work. The RBO team addresses improvements to the physical environment, work climate, recognition and reward systems, and the current level of community involvement and social responsibility. Some examples of projects the RBO team has researched, proposed, presented to leaders for buy-in, and implemented include adding a motorcycle area in a part of their parking lot; adding a lactation center for new mothers; remodeling the cafeteria and improving the menu; working with the City of Long Beach to add a left-turn light when exiting the facility because it was a dangerous intersection; and building a $3 million fitness center; among others.

Boeing's C-17 and other Boeing sites have experienced tremendous success in building and developing high-performing, team-based cultures. However, their success is not based on the culture alone. They have integrated their Rudolph Culture with a new and progressive way to define leadership, a well-established institutional memory that does not change with new leadership or outside circumstance (what we refer to as the Corporate Constitution), and a reward structure that is aligned to the vision, strategies, and culture. We refer to these four criteria as the *Four Pillars of Organizational Greatness*. In other words, for your organization to realize similar results, you must examine the bigger picture, or the system in which your culture resides. We consider the Four Pillars of Organizational Greatness to be like Rudolph's legs. If one leg is lame, broken, or missing, then Rudolph can't run. In any organization, nothing exists in a silo. When you think of your organization, recognize that it is more closely related to a living and breathing organism where everything is literally affected and influenced by everything else. Generating a sustainable, competitive advantage through your people depends on successful integration of all four Pillars.

Chapter 5 Review

- The level of organizational greatness is dependent on how well the Four Pillars are integrated.

- While sometimes difficult to assess, measure, and control, the nontangibles (the people part of the organization) drive all of the tangibles (profits, improvements, and other measurable elements).

- Immediate application of training is critical.

- Happy workers are creative and innovative workers!

- The "Ten Lessons Learned on the Boeing C-17 Journey" reflect the thinking behind the tools used, initiatives introduced, and decisions made during the transformation of the C-17 Program.

REDEFINING LEADERSHIP

Building a high-performing, team-based Rudolph Culture is only possible when it is integrated with the other three Pillars of Organizational Greatness. The second of the Four Pillars is Redefining Leadership. Our intention in this chapter is to provoke thought about how you currently define leadership. More specifically, we want to challenge your thinking and examine how the actual language you use to define leadership can result in your increased ability to create opportunities to lead from wherever you work within your organization. Many books about leadership offer readers a five-steps-to-be-a-leader approach or share a list of characteristics that constitute a good (or great) leader. Many articles and books dissect great leaders throughout history and then leave it up to the reader to put those qualities into action in their own life. However, on our journey, we discovered that if workers, managers, or Rudolphs define leadership as "the person who owns the company I work for" or define leadership as a title or position on the organizational chart, then all of the characteristics in the world will not open their eyes to opportunities to lead from where they are. So, how do *you* define leadership?

Take a moment to write down your definition of leadership. In our leadership training workshops, one of the first exercises we conduct is to have each person write his or her personal definition of leadership. Then, each individual shares that definition with the group, and it does not take long to recognize that each of us defines it from different angles, with different emphases and different characteristics. Rarely, if ever, do two definitions among a group of coworkers read exactly the same. At this point, you may be wondering, what does this have to do with leveraging my Rudolph Factor? In the simplest terms, finding the bright lights that will drive innovation in your business requires your Rudolphs to not only contribute innovative thinking, but also to actually drive the innovation itself. *Driving* implies that somebody takes the wheel—*leading* the process of sharing, reviewing, and implementing creative and innovative ideas into the organization.

Because we believe language is reflective of a person's values, beliefs, attitudes, and thinking, it is important to share our unique definition of leadership. We define leadership as a *commitment to the success of the people around you.* This definition is based on two important realizations made while gathering research about the language of leadership. We asked nearly 700 people two simple questions: (1) What is the one thing that hinders you most from generating an extraordinary product or service, and (2) How do you define leadership? With an almost 50 percent response rate in the first 24 hours, nearly 80 percent of our respondents thought that management or leadership was the single most influential hindrance to extraordinary products and/or services! Also, people who held positions or titles of leader or manager defined leadership as an action or behavior (to inspire others or create a vision were the two most popular responses), while the people doing the work defined leadership as a title or position (the person who leads the team or the person who inspires workers were two common responses). Imagine the implications! Based on the findings, we have positional leaders and managers expecting workers to see opportunities to lead from where they are, and we have workers expecting the leaders and managers to take responsibility for leading. With fingers pointed diametrically at one another, it is no wonder that we have issues with leadership development in most organizations.

In sharing our definition of leadership over the past three years, we have found that it resonates with management and positional leaders *as well as with* workers because it opens the door for *anyone* in an organization to *lead from where they are*, rather than waiting for the executive team or management to "do something." It also generates a greater sense of personal responsibility in workers to lead the organization to its intended vision, which is one of the greatest challenges facing leaders today.

LEADING FROM WHERE YOU ARE

Within the Boeing C-17 Program, it is widely recognized that the story begins and ends with leadership. We are not saying it begins and ends with the *positional leaders or management*—but with a new definition of leadership. From the "Ten Lessons Learned on the Boeing C-17 Journey" revealed in the previous chapter, we are going to address lessons four, five, and nine in this chapter. Lesson nine is also discussed in Chapter 7 as it relates to the development of a Corporate Constitution. To be clear about what leadership means within the Boeing C-17 Program, the former Program Manager, David Bowman, defined it as *connecting people to their future*. This is reflected in Boeing C-17 team training sessions where awareness about the role and responsibilities of leaders is raised. In leading from where they are, Boeing C-17 leaders:

- Are "purveyors of hope" who create the vision and inspire others to achieve it.

- Take others to places they normally would not go alone.
- Encourage an environment where highly creative—and somewhat inherently risky—innovative thinking is welcomed.
- Create an environment supporting peak performance *and* employee satisfaction.
- Must be role models who *walk the talk!*

LESSON FOUR: LEADERS MUST EXECUTE BUSINESS STRATEGIES THROUGH OTHERS

This brings us to the fourth lesson of the "Ten Leadership Lessons Learned"—*leaders must execute business strategies through others ... with the people.* Employees are more personally committed when they are encouraged to define what the business strategies mean to them. In a people-centric Rudolph Culture, similar to the discussion in the last chapter about how training must have immediate application, business strategies must have immediate relevance to people's work. The effective execution of business strategies only occurs through people, and if people do not or cannot determine any relevance to their work, they will not find a compelling enough reason to support the business strategies. Many times, corporations spend a bundle of money, time, and other resources creating business strategies only to have them fall by the wayside when there is no effort demonstrated in the execution phase. Management can point out many reasons for ineffective strategy execution, but unless employees are committed to them, the strategies created will not bear fruit. The following story demonstrates how one Rudolph led from where he was by first recognizing his need for the assistance of many people to initiate and implement quality improvement initiatives aligned to business strategies of improving productivity and reducing costs. After finding other Rudolphs, this small but mighty herd creatively encouraged employees to become engaged enough to transform their factory.

I had the opportunity to be one of the Boeing change agents who initiated the use of "Lean" concepts on the C-17 Program to improve productivity and reduce cost. When we started introducing Lean principles on the C-17 shop floor, we developed detailed strategies and plans, many of which were based on the Toyota Production System.

However, we realized early on that *even the best process designs do not go very far if you do not have the buy-in and engagement of the people who own the processes*. We started to conduct process design workshops, which we call Accelerated Improvement Workshops (AIWs). The AIWs relied on expert knowledge and input of the process owners, and they utilized employee engagement to drive Lean improvements.

This powerful combination of Employee Involvement and Lean helped transform our factory.

Lee Whittington
Director, C-17 Program Performance, The Boeing Company

LESSON FIVE: LEADERSHIP MUST BE PERSISTENT

The fifth lesson—*leadership must be persistent, stay the course, and refuse to give up*—refers to an intentionally designed principle called "Line of Sight," and the tool used to facilitate it is called the Vision Support Plan (VSP). The line-of-sight language refers to the vision and values being aligned with business strategies and supporting objectives throughout the Boeing C-17 Program. In other words, at every layer and level of the Program, supporting objectives are aligned to a small number (two or three) of key business imperatives that can change over time. Employees are highly involved in this process, which ensures a greater level of engagement to fulfill agreed-on objectives. The VSP process aligns goals from the top to the bottom and from the bottom to the top. Anyone can track goals and functions all the way up to the CEO. It is tracked and measured monthly and helps everyone see the light at the end of the tunnel. It is like having the cover of a puzzle box available so that you can see what it looks like when all the pieces are put together. Without the VSP process, each team or area has a piece or two of the puzzle but is stumbling around trying to see to which pieces fit. To facilitate the process, there are VSP focal points and a fairly high level of employee participation.

LESSON NINE: TRADITIONAL ROLES MUST CHANGE

The ninth lesson is that *traditional roles must change (for leaders and team members)*. In Chapter 4 we shared the challenges faced by teams and five things team members must do that are essential to sustaining their cultural revolution. With regard to positional leaders and managers, the constant challenge is to continually engage their people by:

- Being more participative than autocratic
- Asking for collective ideas from people rather than imposing initiatives on people
- Treating all employees as business partners regardless of their title
- Delegating day-to-day decision making
- Focusing on removing barriers and providing resources for people to be successful

Creating awareness of an alternative way of defining leadership organization-wide has contributed to the development of over 500 formal C-17 teams generating millions of dollars of cost savings and cost avoidance from self-initiated projects that go through the Creative Edge Program or Team-Based Business Improvements (TBBI). Can you imagine what your work environment might look like if these five points were already in place within your organization? Consider how your role might change if you did not have to be concerned with having to dictate, watch, measure, and control employees' actions, if you were freed from having to make every little decision, and you were well liked *and* respected for lifting up the people around you, who in turn brought you to new and higher levels of performance.

If this sounds good, here is even better news . . . we discovered through interviews over the past year and a half that Boeing C-17 leaders (*not* positional leaders but those who see opportunities to lead from where they are) are not always born leaders. Although some people's Rudolph space is clearly in the context of leading others, not everyone feels most comfortable in the leadership capacity. As previously mentioned, we believe the language you use is the single most contributing factor to *being* a leader and seeing opportunities to demonstrate leadership capabilities. You do not have to take a number of classes or get a degree in leadership to be a leader. If you define leadership as we do—a commitment to the success of people around you—you can start leading right now!

START LEADING TODAY

Using our AVTAR model, your actions are a manifestation of your thinking. Our thinking most closely resembles the philosophies behind servant leadership, natural leadership, and situational leadership. Information about those specific leadership theories is easy to find. Some thoughts for you to consider: leadership does not exist without people who follow, which requires you to value and revitalize the relationships around you. Effective—even spectacular—leadership has nothing to do with the leader but everything to do with other people and the processes they manage. If you are not on board with this kind of thinking, your actions will feel awkward and forced.

If you recognize this within yourself, all is not lost. The first thing to do is to spend some time reflecting about how you define leadership, consider the language of effective leaders, and what it means to you to lead others before jumping into action. The second recommendation is to facilitate the exercise mentioned in the beginning of this chapter where you have team members, including yourself, take a moment to define leadership. Have each person share his or her definition with everyone to see how uniquely we all view this seemingly simple word. Offer an alternative that allows *anyone to lead from where they are*. Your definition must be phrased with language that speaks to those outside of your organization. Please feel free to use our definition of leadership as "a commitment to the success of people around you."

The next step is pivotal. You must commit yourself to the success of the people around you. Whether you define leadership in this way or not, it is imperative that you are compelled to ensure others' success. If you are unable to do this, or it is not coming quite naturally, we recommend going back to assessing the value of your awareness of effective leadership (the "V" from the AVTAR model). Ask yourself why effective leadership is important. In committing yourself to the success of others, you will be connecting them to their future.

Always be on the lookout for win-wins. When a negotiable issue is presented or raised, be the person who asks "Who wins, and does anyone lose as a result of this decision?" We recommend using the AVTAR model, which we have used to present material throughout this book, to educate the people around you by raising their level of awareness about the language they are using to define leadership:

What kind of results can you expect?

- People around you go above and beyond the call of duty.
- People share the responsibility for the success of the organization.
- People enjoy working together.
- Rudolphs (and non-Rudolphs) generate and contribute creativity and innovations.

- A sustainable competitive advantage is possible.
- Organizational greatness is possible.

The following story from the current Vice President/General Manager of Global Mobility Systems, Jean Chamberlin, speaks to the responsibility leaders must take with regard to helping others find meaning in their work so that there is a direct line of sight between workers' visions and the organizational vision.

My passion has been helping others find the nobility in their everyday work. What is their purpose, and how do they make a difference? For the team that produces, delivers, and sustains the C-17, the affirmation of their purpose is seen almost daily in the newspaper as we witness the lives that are saved and sustained in the multiple missions carried out by the men and women operating this jet and performing their duties in the protection of our freedom, support to humanitarian aid, medical evacuation, and worldwide peacekeeping. Working on the C-17 Program is a great honor. This is a sentiment shared in many Boeing Programs but particularly strong in this Program because the team can see the difference they make each and everyday.

Jean Chamberlin
Vice President/General Manager, Global Mobility Systems,
Integrated Defense Systems, The Boeing Company

With a team-based Rudolph Culture under development and a new way of looking at and defining leadership, we are ready to introduce the third Pillar of Organizational Greatness, the creation of a Corporate Constitution.

Chapter 6 Review

- Language used to define leadership creates opportunities to *lead from where you are.*
- Leadership is a commitment to the success of people around you.
- Role models must walk the talk!
- Business strategies are executed through others... with the people!
- Line of Sight is essential to aligning vision and values to strategies and supporting objectives.

DEVELOPING A CORPORATE CONSTITUTION

The third of the Four Pillars of Organizational Greatness, the development of a Corporate Constitution, involves contributing factors that result in an organization's civil code and political infrastructure, which are generally recalled as institutional memory. In any organization, the "this is the way we do things" concept is reflective of how powerful an organization's institutional memory is and whether the members of that organization will be able to adapt to an ever-changing external environment. In leveraging your Rudolph Factor, the successful development of a Corporate Constitution is dependent on identifying the political system that currently exists within your organization and recognizing whether it is supportive of building a team-based Rudolph Culture. In this chapter, we discuss political structures within organizations, share two more lessons from the Boeing C-17 Program's "Ten Lessons Learned," and finish with ideas and tools to get you started in creating your organization's Corporate Constitution.

POLITICS AS USUAL? NO

Every organization has inherent *and necessary* political systems that exist to create order out of diverse interests, perspectives, and/or goals. While the means to create order may differ (via imposition or collaboration), the management of people and processes is not a neutral endeavor. Politics, in terms of negotiation, coalition, and influence building is commonplace in today's organizational life. Interestingly, when the subject of office politics is introduced, most people respond with disgust—or at the very least, share a negative experience based on office politics. We believe it is still one of the two things our parents tell us not to talk about in mixed company. Kidding aside, it is unfortunate that politics has become such a dirty word because it is a necessary element in every organization. The characteristics that make business politics *good* or *bad* depend on the type of political structure.

In the United States, we govern ourselves in a democracy. However, within the larger national political structure, it is truly amazing to see how many organizations' political structures are more reflective of dictatorships, autocracies, monarchies, or bureaucracies. In our work with companies large and small, we have found that workers are at a distinct disadvantage when the political structure of their organization is not a democracy. While we do not plan to offer a lesson on civics or government, there are several implications of how business politics play a role in day-to-day organizational life. Creating a Corporate Constitution will encourage a non-coercive form of social order and ensure the appropriate political structure is in place for a highly effective, team-based Rudolph Culture to really fly (pun intended).

Imagine the life of a worker who lives in a democratic society, but for five days a week and eight hours a day must obey the orders of a power-hungry boss. The only freedom this worker has is to find another job. While this might appear extreme, you would be shocked at some of the stories of power, control, and authority shared from workers in many different industries, regardless of the size of the company. Perhaps you are beginning to see how the political structure contributes to the disconnection between managers' attempts at eliciting creativity and innovations from workers and the associated lack of employee involvement and contribution as discussed in the first chapter. Your rights as a paid employee should not be fewer than your rights as a citizen living in a democracy.

However, there is an interesting opposition to this perspective. The thinking is that if managers give their employees rights, they will lose their personal power as a manager. As we have shared, more often than not, large organizations are run by command-and-control managers who wield great power over their subordinates based on their position, their capacity to reward and punish, and/or their ability to influence. Most large organizations without a healthy Corporate Constitution in place have strong autocratic tendencies, where the power to influence behaviors rests in the hands of an individual or a small group of individuals. You may be wondering where the source of this perceived power comes from. Some of the sources of perceived power we have recognized include, but are not limited to:

- Formal authority based on title or position
- Control over resources (information, technology, supplies, training, as well as monetary resources) and the scarcer the resources, the greater the perception of power
- Control over the organizational structure, policies, rules, and/or regulations
- Informal authority based on personal characteristics or informal networks

WHAT IS A CORPORATE CONSTITUTION?

In a healthy, politically decentralized and democratic environment, like Boeing's C-17 Program, the Corporate Constitution is the written and unwritten *civil code* that everyone has agreed to abide by and that the infrastructure ensures it is upheld. It is based more on values than rules and includes how members of the organization view and define ethics, civility, collaboration, and boundaries. With a shared purpose in place and values driving thinking and actions, employees have a greater sense of pride in their work and understanding of coworkers' roles. In the most progressive and forward-thinking organizations, a healthy Corporate Constitution is steadfast and does not change over several years, if not decades.

Without a shared purpose and using rules to drive thinking and actions, people employed in autocratic or bureaucratic organizations experience uncertainty, anxiety, and nervousness. Furthermore, the culture becomes a breeding ground for power trips and self-preserving or self-promoting political maneuvering. Rudolphs who work in the capacity of management in a nondemocratic organization must use nontraditional—and sometimes, very creative—methods to survive in a system that demands actions that are contrary to their values and thinking. Again, we offer the Corporate Constitution as a structure to provide boundaries from within the organization's culture functions.

When everyone in an organization is "on the same page" and compelled to lead from where they are, developing a Corporate Constitution is a natural process. In the Boeing C-17 Program, there is an understanding that their Rudolph Culture is a natural outcome of the strength of their Constitution. Their culture is continually affected by every interaction and transaction between every person every day and with every process they manage. In democratic organizations, such as theirs, power is exercised through highly participative methods where everyone is encouraged to share in the management process. This is not to say that there are no managers who attempt to wield power or no power-hungry people. They exist in the best of democratic organizations; however, their abilities to take control *over others* is limited due to the political structure, the team-based Rudolph Culture, the language used to define leadership, and a reward structure that encourages democracy and win-wins rather than self-promotion. The following story from a C-17 production mechanic and team lead illustrates how everybody benefits from participatory-based management.

We have been able to take ownership of our work because of C-17's "team" concept. Teams are more in control of their destiny now. Before the transformation, ideas were dictated down from the top. Now we move the ideas up from the workers. It helps with innovation and the feeling that we are part of the bigger picture. Our ideas are worth something, and we are putting them to work. Even after years of improvements, we are still implementing new ideas. It benefits everybody! We directly impact the product and get rewarded for it.

Craig Johnson
Production Mechanic/Team Lead, Wing Support C-17, The Boeing Company

In any healthy political structure, people in formal positions of power or influence are accountable to a process of checks and balances. In an organization, checks and balances generally present themselves as opposition to status quo or through valued Rudolphs who can safely ask "Why?" without fearing repercussions. In a culture where everyone takes part in the decision-making process, it becomes quite difficult, if not impossible, for anyone to oppose decisions. Similarly, if you choose not to vote in an election, you also lose the right to complain about whomever is elected.

Some organizations offer a limited ability for participation because they are not comfortable "handing over" power and control to employees. In this case, employees are allowed to make minor decisions, but when push comes to shove, their opinions are not valued. As seen with Boeing C-17, a handing over of power and responsibility requires new kinds of training to give employees the skills and tools to self-manage. The development of a healthy and effective Corporate Constitution ensures a steadfast approach to sustaining Boeing C-17's highly successful Rudolph Culture into their future no matter what external circumstances are presented, which leads us to the seventh lesson—*You must have a written plan.*

LESSON SEVEN: YOU MUST HAVE A WRITTEN PLAN

The seventh lesson, *you must have a written plan*, refers to ensuring that the Corporate Constitution is supported with quantitative data tracking forward movement of teams.

Because we are suggesting the creation of a Corporate Constitution that is reflective of a democratic organizational political structure, we must be certain that the organization's senior executives and midlevel management support a people-centric vision and aim. At Boeing C-17, the general political structure is modeled after a democracy and is used as the primary method by which divergent ideas, goals, thinking, strategies, vision, and values converge. The Corporate Constitution is the documented system of fundamental principles according to which the organization is governed. Without these values and thinking, the organization cannot survive.

In the C-17 Program, the Corporate Constitution is aligned to other documents including the Vision Support Plan (VSP), Team-Based Business Improvements (TBBI), and the Employee Involvement Team Management System. These are three of their "best practices tools" used to quantify forward movement. The VSP (which is primarily used in the Integrated Defense Systems business unit) includes critical milestones, the name of the person responsible, and a schedule of time lines and due dates. While it is one thing to have a document in place that inspires democratic thinking and behaviors, it is something far greater to track and measure it. The other tool used is a TBBI template. It contains information about self-initiated, team-based projects including:

- Team maturity stage.
- Project status.

- Team members.
- How the project improves the team's business.
- Methods and tests used to identify improvement opportunities.
- The team's action plan.
- The potential to be a process/system change.
- How the team's business was improved.
- Cost savings/avoidance.
- How the project improved the team *and* customer satisfaction.
- Return on Investment (ROI)—however, this is optional.

In large organizations, the importance of having efficient ways of documenting the work that teams do to improve their part of the business cannot be overstated. The delicate balance lies in providing ways to document that are not overly bureaucratic or command and control. One way that Boeing C-17 has addressed this issue is the use of an electronic database for the teaming process. The system was initially developed by a workforce team at one of C-17's sister facilities in Palmdale. Known as Employee Involvement Team Management System (EITMS), the web-based tool helps teams manage their team business quickly, efficiently, and effectively.

EITMS was developed with input from EI Practitioners and tested with real teams at multiple Boeing sites. The approach used in the design phase of the system was critical because it provided an opportunity to get input from the workforce. The main components of EITMS include: team rosters, charters, empowerment plans, team training modules, effective meeting management, lean plans, customer surveys, and TBBI projects. The system is designed to be team driven with minimal oversight by management, enabling the sustainment of workforce empowerment. EITMS has quickly become the common team management system used across Boeing and has become a part of the company's formal goals. After the companywide launch in 2007, over 4,000 formal teams have started using EITMS to help manage their teams' business. The following story depicts how a system developed to track team efforts in a Rudolph Culture inspires greater collaboration across the Boeing enterprise.

I have been able to watch the growth of EITMS from the initial homegrown platform built by an EI team in the High Desert to the deployment of the online enterprise system. All along the way I've marveled at how quickly it has been adopted by programs and teams across the company. Even though I had the vision that it would be a great tool, it has still been amazing to watch. I think a key to the growth of EITMS is the thought that was put into the design phase of the tool. Terra Kruse, the original EITMS Project Lead, was intentional about involving EI Practitioners and real teams in the process. She utilized the expertise available across the company—the people that work with teams day in and day out in order to build a tool that could actually work for the teams. There was also a lot of thought put into designing a system that would provide the opportunity for teams to collaborate with a level of structure that isn't overly complicated or cumbersome.

Another key feature of the system is that it provides teams across the company the ability to share project ideas in a fast and efficient manner. Teams love to see what other teams across the company are doing—it drives the vision of Boeing being one company! From my perspective, EITMS is a successful tool because most people want the opportunity to work together to positively impact their part of the business, and it allows them a chance to do that.

Suzi Hammond-Miller
Employee Involvement Practitioner, C-17 Program, The Boeing Company

AMENDING THE CONSTITUTION

Have you ever heard the phrase, "It'll take an act of Congress"? Amending an organization's Corporate Constitution should be considered with ample degree of thought and input from a variety of sources. Like a government's constitution, the power in the document is that it ensures checks and balances. If the Corporate Constitution was to change willy-nilly, or with every new CEO, neither management nor the workers would take it very seriously.

LESSON NINE: TRADITIONAL ROLES MUST CHANGE

With a steadfast, democratic Corporate Constitution in place, the ninth lesson, *traditional roles must change*, could not have more relevance. Within the Boeing C-17 Program, through trial and error, they have clearly identified how every person's role is immediately affected. Each person must behave as if the desired results—or goals—have already been achieved. Otherwise, people can wait forever to find "the right time" to change. For example, if at a meeting on Thursday night we all decide to create a goal to be a world-class organization, behaviors must demonstrate that immediately...yes, that night. For this to be possible, all people must identify how being a world-class organization immediately affects their role and share that with the team. In other words, if I am not world class now, what does it look like, sound like, and feel like to be world class tomorrow? Does anything change? Am I already thinking and behaving in a way that demonstrates *what it means to me* to be world class? Do my internal and external customers feel as if my current thinking and behaviors are supportive of a world-class organization? Please recognize this is a very personal process, which collectively has a profound effect on business results and achieving desired outcomes.

For the Boeing C-17 Program to continue to be successful, the executive team, managers, and workers are *always* committed to improving business results, *always* focusing on continuous process improvements, and *always* keeping the customer (internal and external) in mind. This would be included in their Corporate Constitution. Please note the absolute language of *always*—the Program's very existence could be in jeopardy if any element is compromised. The following story demonstrates how every individual of the organization is responsible for upholding the Constitution and sustaining the improved culture.

Our culture has transformed from one where employees would check in at the door as a number to actually contributing to the business. People experience pride when they are able to have their voice and input heard. It's good for the union environment because it helps create a culture with the right people doing the right job and having the help they need when they need it. It also enables Rudolphs to come out into the open and flourish.

Because we have EI written into our union contract (constitution), the union and management both hold themselves accountable to the principles of involvement and empowerment. This written language ensures an environment of working together to sustain a partnership and find win-win solutions to our business needs.

Once the workers feel ownership of their business and a connection to their future, there is no turning
(*continued*)

(continued)
back. The workforce will challenge leadership to sustain the improved culture, and the best leadership will respond with a greater vision for the future.

Arlene Rios,
UAW Employee Involvement Representative, International UAW

More specifically, they have identified behaviors to managers and workers in supporting the Corporate Constitution.

Managers must
- Communicate a clear vision to employees.
- Train and empower workers to make sound business decisions.
- Ask employees to be fully involved and engaged.
- Relinquish any perception of control as the team grows more capable of taking on more self-management functions.
- Be responsible for recognizing and publicizing progress and successes.

Workers must
- Recognize that with more responsibility comes more accountability.
- Take on more ownership of the day-to-day decision making as their skill set grows.

- Be responsible for sharing information and supporting each other.
- Elevate real or perceived problems to the team and management as soon as they are recognized.

ELEMENTS OF YOUR CORPORATE CONSTITUTION

Your Constitution should address all sectors of your business, no matter how diversified the organization is, and it should drive the AVTAR process for each employee (meaning, the Corporate Constitution raises Awareness, places Value on the awareness, influences each person's Thinking, which drives appropriate Actions that Result in the organization's desired outcome). The level of credibility and success is directly related to how well it is documented, communicated, and demonstrated by leadership *all the time*. If senior leadership is abiding by the Corporate Constitution, everyone else will, too. Elements that make up a comprehensive and powerful Corporate Constitution include:

- *Mission or aim:* What does your organization intend to collectively accomplish?
- *Vision:* How do you see the organization fitting into the larger society?
- *Brand promise:* An expression of your organization's commitment to deliver on your product(s) and/or service(s).

- *Values:* Those things that guide the collective thinking, actions, and decision making.

- *Financial goals:* (Not created haphazardly and not to come at the cost of something else in the system.)

- *Civil code:* Five to ten very specific points the collective organization does to achieve desired outcomes (ways of working together). These could include things the organization is committed to, how people are valued, the organization's commitment to innovative thinking, risk taking from employees, and so on.

While the content of Corporate Constitutions may differ based on unique values and visions of varying organizations, we have strong recommendations as well as some examples for your review. First and foremost, when the Constitution is being created, recognize those aspects that people within the organization would be unwilling to compromise on no matter who is leading or what circumstances may be present in the future. Also, recognize that the language used in the Constitution makes the path less of a destination and more of a journey. Developing the language in a Corporate Constitution should not be an annual event, nor one that is specifically revisited whenever the senior leader changes. In fact, succession planning should include potential candidates' ability to uphold the elements of the Corporate Constitution. Finally, participation of senior leaders, managers, and employees is critical in ensuring that everyone will uphold the Constitution. EI Practitioner Richard Nicholson suggests developing a communication plan from leadership. Nicholson suggests drafting a letter by a senior leader and sending it to everyone thanking them for their hard work and increased involvement. The letter would also explain the process by which a steering committee would be formed and asks that everyone participate. Employees need to know their ideas are important and pivotal to the success of the organization. With the team-based Rudolph Culture in place at C-17, such forms of communication from senior leadership are powerful and inspiring ways to encourage involvement early on.

While many organizations have a mission statement, vision, and set of values, workers tend to disconnect when they do not see these elements in action. If workers believe the mission, vision, and values are simply *lip service*, the Corporate Constitution will not encourage people to think or behave any differently than they currently are. We highly recommend the vision be *no less than 20 years* out as it will ensure creative and innovative thinking beyond current issues and opportunities. We also recommend stating the vision as if it exists now. Consider the subtle, yet powerful difference between the following two visions: *We will work together to be a global enterprise for aerospace leadership* versus *People working together as a global enterprise for aerospace leadership.* The second vision is The Boeing Company's Vision 2016 and is stated in such a way that they are already working together as an enterprise, whereas the first vision leaves "working together" to some undetermined time in the future with, *We will....* Using words such as, *will, will be, going to be* leave us asking the question "When?" When will you start working together? We know the difference is subtle, but it makes a profound difference in how people internalize the language and turn the vision into reality.

An example of an effective and timeless vision statement created for the Boeing C-17 Engineering Team in 1998 follows.

People are passionate about their work and making a future for the Program.
An environment where people feel

- Valued;
- That their ideas matter and opinions count;
- That they have an affect on a shared destiny.

An environment where people feel

- Diversity is appreciated;
- People's creativity is maximized and respected;
- Everyone has something to offer—authorship.

Dr. Katherine Erlick
Director of Mission Assurance, IDS Engineering, The Boeing Company

In considering the language used in constructing the Corporate Constitution, recognize that the infrastructures and systems that emphasize centralization encourage command-and-control behaviors, while decentralization is more reflective of democratic behaviors. When contemplating what values are of significance, it may be helpful to think of those characteristics that are absolutes—those things that must always occur. Another company that provides an excellent example of an effective set of values for a Corporate Constitution—although they do not call it that . . . yet—is Southwest Airlines.

Craig worked with Southwest Airlines for nearly 10 years, and he recalls from his perspective those characteristics that he believes were absolutes to be internalized by everyone in the organization. These include but are not limited to:

- Always have fun.
- Always value smart work.
- Always value every person and their thinking, however unconventional it might appear (value Rudolphs).
- Always value every contribution.
- Always value open communication.
- Always value external competition because internal competition is a tremendous waste of resources.
- Always value a positive work ethic.

- Always value people going above and beyond the call of duty because it is their choice to do so.
- Always value people for who they are.

We believe this is a great template to start with and personalize specifically for your organization's needs. Southwest Airlines operates across 64 cities, and each has its own unique culture but follows the same underlying Corporate Constitution.

FINAL THOUGHTS ON CORPORATE CONSTITUTIONS

We believe the Corporate Constitution can be the glue that holds people together, and this has never been as important as it is now in our current global financial crisis. The larger or more global the organization, the more important the Constitution becomes. It is the rudder for guiding the ship to new possibilities, opportunities, and completely new frontiers in business. We also believe that as the larger Corporate Boeing begins to transform from a product-based model that encourages silos and separateness to a needs-based model that encourages all 160,000 Boeing employees across 70 countries work together to create new (and fulfill unknown future needs) of commercial travel, defense systems, and space exploration—the strength of their Corporate Constitution will be pivotal to its continued success.

Chapter 7 Review

- Business politics (which facilitate the convergence of divergent goals and interests) are not the same as office politics (which are power games that result in resource drains).

- A well-designed Rudolph Culture encourages the political structure that people operate within.

- Is your organization's political structure reflective of a democracy, autocracy, monarchy, bureaucracy, or dictatorship?

- The political structure occurs by design or default. There is a choice.

- The larger and more layered an organization is, the more essential is the Corporate Constitution.

CREATING AN ALTERNATIVE AND ALIGNED REWARD STRUCTURE

The last of the Four Pillars of Organization Greatness, an Aligned Reward Structure, is the most complex and least understood by most managers. We believe there is an incredible opportunity to revolutionize how organizations motivate *and* reward their employees. Along our journey, we have discovered the things used to *reward* employees are not the same mechanisms that *motivate* or inspire. To further complicate the issue, *one size does not fit all* when it comes to recognizing, rewarding, or motivating employees. For example, while some might feel recognized and motivated with monetary rewards, Rudolphs often find greater reward in seeing their ideas in action. In the C-17 Program, this became clear when the Engineering EI steering team decided to survey what rewards their engineers would value. Historically, rewards had come in the form of mugs and jackets and such. When the results from the survey were reviewed, the committee found the engineers were interested in growing intellectually. The reward they most desired and valued was receiving funding to attend classes and conferences.

In this last chapter, we first distinguish between motivation and reward and offer insights on how to ensure the reward structure is actually perceived by employees as a reward. We also revisit each of the four modes of operation (tactical, facilitative, creative, and visionary) as defined in Chapter 3 and offer our perspectives and tools regarding what people in each mode find inspiring and what is typically perceived as a worthy and valued reward. Finally, we share another one of Boeing C-17's "Top Ten Lessons"—lesson eight, *recognition must be part of the process*.

DO REWARDS INSPIRE?

It is most important to first distinguish between the terms *motivation* and *reward*. Many managers are trained to use rewards to motivate workers to work harder, which may not be an accurate perception, particularly in a

Rudolph Culture. We believe the technical term is *positive reinforcement*—using some form of reward to reinforce those behaviors you want to see continued. Conversely, when discouraging certain behaviors, many managers rely on the theory of negative reinforcement. While this may work when raising a child or training a pet, it does nothing to encourage or elicit creative and innovative thinking from employees, particularly when the reward given is not considered of value to the recipient.

Understanding the psychology of reward and motivation for each of the four modes (tactical, facilitative, creative, and visionary) is one of the biggest challenges that every manager faces. And because most managers are responsible for conducting a formal performance evaluation process with employees, which tend to be fairly ineffective, it only makes their task more challenging. As we have discovered, to be successful in leveraging an organization's Rudolph Factor, a healthy Corporate Constitution provides the framework from which a team-based Rudolph Culture can operate. And within which appropriate and valued motivation tactics and reward structures are exercised.

For example, the level of EI realized at the Boeing C-17 Program is further encouraged by a reward structure that is fair, timely, and consistent. Also of significant importance is that if the reward structure does not support the other three Pillars of Organizational Greatness (establishing a Rudolph Culture, redefining leadership, and developing a Corporate Constitution), actions and behaviors *will not change*. People always behave *perfectly within the reward structure* created for them. (W. Edwards Deming's thinking and recommendations revolved around this notion that the system is more of a driver of individual behaviors than the individuals themselves.)

For example, we worked with a small company in the construction industry having performance issues with their salespeople. When asked what the pay structure looked like, the response was, "100 percent salary." The owners were interested in upholding their reputation of excellent quality of services. However, this structure was not motivating the salespeople to work harder with the downturn of construction. Whether or not they made a sale was of no consequence to the sales team—unless the members of the sales team were committed to the success of the greater organization beyond their own personal financial success. We asked the owners if they thought that behaviors might change if they switched the pay structure to 100 percent commission, half salary/half commission, or to a shared commission between the three salespeople. As we discussed each scenario, it was clear each structure would elicit different behaviors—and not all scenarios would necessarily improve current conditions. The point of the discussion was to raise the consciousness of the owners to how their "system" was influencing the behaviors of their salespeople. This awareness inspired a dialogue between the owners and the salespeople regarding the current system and what options might result in closer alignment with company's financial goals for the sales team as well as for the rest of the organization.

MOTIVATING AND REWARDING THE FOUR MODES OF OPERATION

As previously discussed, we believe there are four distinct modes of operation (tactical/operational, facilitative/managerial, creative/innovative, and visionary/strategic). These modes do not necessarily coincide with a person's title or position on the organizational chart. Rudolphs, who are naturally creative and innovative in their work environment, can be found in any job function including frontline worker, salesperson, manager, accountant, executive, janitor, or any other capacity found in an organization. Starting with the tactical and operational mode, the motivating feature of their work is that it tends to be a means to another end. They "plug-and-chug" so they can do whatever strikes their fancy away from work. Again, there is nothing positive or negative about this mode of operation, and it is highly essential to organizations. However, as a manager, it is most helpful to know their primary motivator tends to be having consistent work in a pleasant and agreeable environment. The type of reward most desired and appreciated tends to be monetary in form, including bonuses, flexibility in scheduling, time off, or cash rewards.

The second mode—facilitative and managerial—tends to find the greatest inspiration or motivation in gaining prestige or receiving positive acknowledgment from senior leadership or from workers. In most traditional organizations, we believe managers are caught in a system that closely resembles the childhood board game Chutes and Ladders. If you are not familiar with the game, the theme involves children climbing ladders or sliding down chutes. The idea behind the game is to teach behavioral ethics as the artwork depicts squares on the bottom of the ladders showing a child doing a good deed, and the top of the ladder shows the child enjoying the reward. Conversely, at the top of the chutes, the artwork depicts children behaving with mischief, and the pictures at the bottom of the chute show the child suffering the consequences. We believe many managers are unknowingly stuck in this *game* and subsequently are thinking and acting in such a way to get up the ladder as quickly as possible. Managers often hide or do not fully disclose problems or deficiencies because they perceive something "bad" happening could be a direct ticket to a chute. In the world of middle management, there are relatively few demotions—instead, they are moved laterally or moved out of the organization altogether.

We believe this is a horribly ineffective system and one of the main reasons managers can be a primary obstacle to leveraging an organization's Rudolph Factor. Through the eyes of a manager, a Rudolph's contribution is not considered creative and innovative, but rather nontraditional and unconventional . . . and very risky to a manager's long-term success. Often, a Rudolph's thinking and actions appear way too risky for the predicament or position many managers are in. Therefore, understanding that managers in a healthy organization like Boeing C-17 are motivated by internal acknowledgment from their subordinates and senior leaders is a good start for creating a better environment for managers to operate effectively.

For our third mode, creative and innovative Rudolphs, we discovered their greatest incentive for motivation is having an outlet to contribute unconventional thinking—having a voice—as well as being empowered to execute innovative ideas without the fear of repercussion. Rudolphs revealed that the greatest *reward* experienced is the feeling they get in seeing their ideas in action . . . what we refer to as leaving their "hoofprints" throughout the organization. In other words, Rudolphs are motivated by being empowered to make a difference for the organization and rewarded when they see a positive difference has been made via their contribution.

Unique to their counterparts, Rudolphs tend to be less inspired or motivated by short-term monetary incentives or personal gain. Their innovative, call-to-action thinking comes very naturally to them. As previously discussed, many Rudolphs typically have a history of multiple negative experiences in "just being themselves" and very purposefully fly below the radar. Their noses can shine again, but only when it is safe to do so. It is possible to leverage your Rudolph Factor when the leadership, culture, and reward structure are aligned to embrace creative and innovative thinking—*and* its inherent risk. The following story is an example of what a Rudolph reward might look like.

As a first level manager, I inherited a team comprised of three different groups of people who historically had been conditioned to mistrust and dislike each other (intensely).... And to top it off, we were co-located after sitting in three different buildings.... Just imagine the tension.... This was about the time that Employee Involvement was being implemented in the office areas. Honestly, I didn't think we had anything to lose; it couldn't get worse! And so we began our journey....

Our first meeting stands out in my mind. After about 20 minutes, one of my more vocal team members (who had tried to get out of going to the conference room in the first place) uttered a strong expletive and stormed out of the room.... I was mortified and discouraged.... But we stayed the course ... and the next time someone criticized the process, I didn't offer to correct the person's attitude because another teammate took care of it. In a very respectful way, she said she disagreed, because in their previous ways of doing business they would not have even been in a room together, let alone been civil and trusting. That is when the facilitator surreptitiously passed me a note saying "It works!" I smiled and knew that we were on the right path.

Coming from a huge success with Employee Involvement on the C-17 Program, I had the opportunity to work with teammates in our General Procurement organization at other sites through my involvement on the People Team. I kept talking about what we did at our site regarding people interaction, process improvements, and so on. Many on the team responded enthusiastically—they wanted what we had! That led the team leader and me to great opportunities to travel to other sites to train the principals of Employee Involvement and/or set up contacts with a local EI focal to start them on their own journeys. It was a very exciting time.

Elizabeth Haseltine
EI Focal—Supplier Management, The Boeing Company

The last mode, the visionary and strategic mode, finds the greatest motivation from external acknowledgment. This typically comes in the form of positive publicity from a third party or outside source—being invited to speak at a conference, being invited to be a board member for a charitable organization their organization fosters, or other external sources of validation. The greatest reward experienced is leaving a legacy through their work in the organization. We have summarized the specific motivators and rewards in Table 8.1.

Table 8.1 Operational Modes and Rewards

Mode of Operation	Tactical or Operational	Facilitative or Managerial	Creative or Innovative	Visionary or Strategic
Motivator	Job is a means to another end	Potential to climb the corporate ladder	Potential to make a positive difference for the organization	External acknowledgment
	Having consistent work in an agreeable environment	More freedom with their team(s)	Having a voice to share thinking	Positive publicity
		Looking good to senior leadership	Having a safe environment in which to be themselves	Potential to leave a legacy with organization
		Acknowledgment from staff or workers	Getting skills necessary to make a greater contribution	Potential to make a difference in the larger society through product(s) and service(s)
Reward	Monetary	Promotion	Seeing their ideas in action	External awards
	Flexible scheduling	Internal award	Training	Healthy functioning organization
	Bonuses	Recognition from senior leaders	Recognition from peers and direct manager	Impact of product or service on society
	Cash rewards		Leaving hoofprints—indelible marks on the organization	

LESSON EIGHT: RECOGNITION MUST BE PART OF THE PROCESS

In the Boeing C-17 Program, managers want to take their work with employee involvement and engagement to the next level where all employees are contributing at their full potential to their team and through personal development. Their vision of "People and Products Making a Difference for Our Customers through Teamwork" is at the very heart of what motivates the entire Boeing C-17 Team. As previously mentioned, there are over 500 formal teams in the Program and approximately 4,500 formal teams in the Integrated Defense Systems Business Unit working on a plethora of problems, processes, and performance management issues with all teams working toward the shared purpose of making a difference for customers and the larger society. At the crux of graduating to the next level of performance are *motivation, rewards*, and *recognition.*

Lesson eight from "Ten Lessons Learned"—*Recognition must be part of the process*—refers to the depth that management values the capacity to lead from wherever you are within the organization. The balancing act between meeting demands of the current global business environment and creating a future every day requires management team members to be advocates of employee engagement. The intangibles, as discussed in Chapter 1, including information, collective knowledge, and employees' commitment to the Program are the lifeblood of Boeing's C-17 Program. Managers understand

and appreciate the underlying philosophy that one size does not fit all when it comes to reward and recognition. Along their journey, they discovered that it is of the utmost importance to have wide and varied means of rewarding employees. In addition to a breadth of rewards, they also have created multiple levels of awards to recognize a job well done. For example, *Pride@Boeing* offers employees multiple ways to acknowledge and appreciate coworkers, contractors, and even customers for good work. Currently, there is an effort to connect the Creative Edge Program to the *Pride@Boeing* Program for the purposes of creating more win-wins for employees and the C-17 Program.

A more formal appreciation honors those who exceed expectations, and achievement recognition acknowledges substantial improvements to products or processes. It is not always easy for a manager to take the time to show his or her appreciation for the little things, but within the C-17 Program there really is no alternative. It is simply that important. Managers and team leaders at Boeing C-17 place such a significant *V*alue on reward and recognition, that it does not escape their *T*hinking, which in turn leads to having a variety of quick and easy ways to say "Thanks!" Little thank-yous mean a great deal to the people receiving them.

For example, they have "Director Giveaways," "Lunch on Us," and "Moose Munchies"—all of which are fun, simple, and frequent informal tangible ways to say "thank you" in a timely and efficient manner. It might include lunch or special treat coupons from the cafeteria. Safety awards are given on a regular basis to teams and individuals exhibiting particular concern for safety, and "Safety Bingo" is an ongoing safety game with prizes to encourage all-points safety requirements. There are also a number of team awards given frequently and regularly to minimize any "scarcity mentality" related to rewards. Because the culture and leadership are healthy, having many types of frequent rewards does not minimize the value of the rewards.

To ensure that employees are properly rewarded, the EI Program Administrator coordinates reward and recognition requirements through a designated recognition focal point person from each Integrated Defense Systems (IDS)—Long Beach, Integrated Performance Team, and site tenant. This includes sites in addition to the Boeing C-17 Program. Literally thousands of "Lunch on Us" and "Moose Munchies" coupons are purchased every year. As you may have guessed, funds for reward and recognition are actually part of the financial budget each year, rather than an afterthought as in most traditional organizations.

Another reward program, called "The Doing Something Right Program," is completely managed by a team of employees and allows teammates to recognize and show their appreciation to subordinates, peers, and supervisors for hard work and effective interpersonal skills. It is a monthly celebration acknowledging contributions of individuals and teams that improve quality, increase on-the-job safety, effectively remove Foreign Object Debris

(FOD), and demonstrate exemplary performance. This Program has also recognized thousands of IDS employees over the past 13 years. Regarded as one of the more "celebrated" Programs, every year the C-17 Program sponsors a float in the Christmas Parade in Long Beach, California. Winners of the "Doing Something Right Program" and their families (approximately 100 to 200 people) are invited to march alongside or ride on the Boeing C-17 float and are given sweatshirts, flashing buttons, and other hoopla for the festivities. It is a remarkable way to reward great work, and it is especially well regarded because families are also able to participate.

One of the most unique features we discovered within the C-17 Program was that "local" and empowered people are supposed to reward and recognize others. Because of the culture, the definition of leadership, and the Corporate Constitution, managers—and employees—are able to create their own team awards and rewards for work well done. Senior management does not mandate it, and it is not an "office politics" scenario. We found the rewards and recognition programs and practices (whether formal or ad hoc) to be genuine, of value to the recipients, and really made the environment a desirable place to work. For example, 2009 will denote the Third Annual Team Appreciation Day. All of IDS (Business Unit) can attend, which translates to approximately 8,000 people. One of the bays in the facility is blocked off, and they have lunch together. Teams can create a storyboard to share the good work they have been doing over the past year. All teams are recognized for their contribution to the success of the organization. Even in these tight economic times, this event is included in the budget because reward and recognition is another essential core value. Just because times are tough does not mean it is okay to stop recognizing people's efforts. In fact, there could not be a better time to inject new energy and enthusiasm into the organization's journey.

With regard to motivation tools, "Gainsharing" is one of the incentive programs used to motivate employees to increase performance by offering an opportunity to share in the profits gained by employee-influenced cost reductions. In this case, The Airlift & Tanker Program/Long Beach Division (which includes Boeing C-17 in addition to other Boeing Programs in Long Beach). The UAW International Union and UAW Local 148 collaborated to create the Gainsharing reward system for Boeing's C-17 and 717 Programs in 1996. It is based on cost reductions made by UAW members and has benefited the company and the union with a payout split of 50/50 on all cost reductions, increased productivity, and ultimately has resulted in delivering a better quality product to their customers.

Everything has its moment in time, so has Gainsharing. The world was changing in the 1980s and early 1990s, bringing with it changes and some hard realities. The United Automobile Aerospace and Agricultural

(continued)

(*continued*)

Implement Workers of America (UAW), along with the UAW Local 148 and the McDonnell Douglas Corporation were jointly facing an urgent need to find ways to reduce cost and improve productivity and quality. We were facing massive layoffs and restructuring. These events highlighted the need for us to work together collaboratively to build a better future for all employees and the company. Further we also were facing greater global competition from abroad.

Out of this scenario was born Employee Involvement and the Gainsharing Program. Employee Involvement was the vehicle and Gainsharing was a tool and incentive utilized to unleash the power and innovation of our teams to lower cost and increase quality and productivity. Gainsharing provided the "skin in the game" for the production workers to justify their involvement, by rewarding them for their efforts with a 50 percent share of the savings. This program existed and thrived from 1995 until December of 2008. In its 13 years of existence the Gainsharing Program has paid out an average amount of just over $1,000 per person each year.

Today going into 2009 and forward we have developed and implemented a new plan called the Employee Performance Program (EPP). After thoroughly reviewing and assessing the merits of the Gainsharing Program, the UAW and the Boeing Company agreed to close the Gainsharing Program and introduce a the new EPP incentive plan. The new EPP provides for a greater alignment of metrics that support the business and drive actions that increase the quality, reduce overall cost, and reinforce Employee Involvement. I believe that the line of sight created by EPP will dramatically improve our business results and increase the earnings potential for our represented employees.

P. James Drake
UAW Employee Performance Program Coordinator, The Boeing Company

One of the most creative incentives for inspiring and motivating continued exemplary performance can be found through Boeing's educational reimbursement program. It is the best we have come across in our work with large organizations. Every employee has the opportunity to grow and learn personally, which in turn, furthers the collective knowledge base. Virtually all expenses are paid for (tuition, books, and fees), as long as it is an accredited university. There are even opportunities to attend other programs such as Dale Carnegie Training. Education is one of the core values to The Boeing Company and is highly encouraged. On any given night, there are approximately 35,000 Boeing employees (enterprise-wide) attending classes. This translates to an "investment" of nearly $100 million per year for tuition reimbursement. Many employees we interviewed shared stories of how they were able to take advantage of ongoing learning opportunities to better themselves and the organization. This is a great win-win for everyone and has long-lasting effects on loyalty and commitment, which only increases the level of engagement by employees.

Chapter 8 Review

- Recognize the difference between recognition, reward, and motivation.

- Not all Rudolphs eat carrots—one size does not fit all when it comes to rewarding your people.

- Some rewards can actually de-incentivize or demotivate employees (if not appreciated or desired by a particular mode of operation—tactical/operational, facilitative/managerial, creative/innovative, or visionary/strategic).

- People tend to operate perfectly within the political structure and systems that have been created—whether by design or by default.

- Are "Chutes and Ladders" happening within your organization? If so, consider altering the system that managers operate within via an alternative and aligned reward structure.

GO FORTH—
AWAKEN THE
RUDOLPH
WITHIN

As we have discussed throughout the story of the Boeing C-17's cultural revolution, from the beginning, senior leadership and management must be committed to a people-centric culture—as opposed to a product-only or process-only focused culture. You simply cannot have products or processes without people, and you must trust your people to do their jobs well. And let's face it, what is the point of it all if we cannot enjoy it along the way! Even with everything in place—a high-performing team-based Rudolph Culture, a progressive way of defining leadership so that anyone can find opportunities to lead from where they are, a healthy Corporate Constitution, and a reward structure that is aligned to the other three Pillars of Organizational Greatness—the Boeing C-17 Program still faces the same challenges and global challenges every other company faces. Like every other organization, they have internal conflict, divergent agendas, goals and ideas all pulling resources and energy in a variety of directions. The difference, and what makes their journey so compelling, is how they process through the issues more effectively than most companies of any size.

It is impossible not to recognize and appreciate how far they have come in such a relatively short amount of time. In our studies within Boeing and other innovative companies, we found that it takes more than a new or unique set of skills to sustain a Rudolph Culture once it is developed. We believe a *system to* identify, nurture, and leverage Rudolphs (those uniquely creative and involuntary agents of change) continues to be the missing link in the quest for sustainable competitive advantage. In supplying this missing link, *The Rudolph Factor* is not simply a new tool or skill set; nor is it just another new leadership or management style or a repackaged but familiar improvement initiative or set of performance criteria. *The Rudolph Factor* embraces all current *and future* performance tools, techniques, initiatives, and criterion because it requires a shift in awareness and thinking that drives a change in actions and behaviors. *The Rudolph Factor* shows how the fabric of extraordinary innovation is actually woven.

Ironically and sadly, the small percentage of employees who have the natural ability to drive and sustain a company's competitive advantage is the one segment of the corporate population that is first to walk out the door day after day. However, when properly nurtured and leveraged, Rudolphs will remain and can deliver remarkable results. For example, in Boeing's C-17 Program, these are ordinary people collectively generating extraordinary ideas.

It is impossible to accurately compute the negative financial impact companies suffer by not retaining their most cost-effective and nonrenewable resource—their innovative people. The progressive business leaders of today are waking up to the cost of losing talent and increasingly understand their products and services will not survive without innovative people—those who can build and implement creative knowledge to create a customer experience that is better than the competitions'. As Boeing's Employee Involvement Office Practitioners, Charlie Macias and Rich Nicholson have shared with us on many occasions, "The real magic is in the people." At a time when the leading edge of the baby-boomer generation is exiting the corporate workforce and an entirely new type of worker—Generation Y or "Millennials"— enters the scene, talent management is taking on a whole new meaning and set of challenges. We believe that there is a much larger percentage of Rudolphs entering the workforce; so the information gleaned here is not only essential to business success, it is timely as well.

LESSON TEN: ENJOY THE JOURNEY!

The tenth (and final) lesson from the "Ten Lessons Learned"—to *enjoy the journey*—comes from the realization that although the Boeing C-17 Program has come a long way, and everyone is extremely proud of their collective accomplishments, they still have a long way to go. The journey continues. They plan to be around for a long time, and in doing so, have to continue to redefine who they are and what constitutes their sustainable competitive advantage in the global marketplace. We believe an advantage is only competitive when it is sustainable over an extended length of time. What most organizations consider a competitive advantage—such as price or quality—is generally not sustainable over time or market conditions.

Currently, many organizations tend to focus on internal improvements or innovation as independent events. For example, there is an incredible focus on introducing the latest process improvement strategies to reduce the cost of doing business. Most initiatives supporting improvement or innovation are used as destination points, rather than launching pads supporting a journey to achieve ongoing organizational greatness. This narrow, events-based thinking does not allow sustainable competitive advantage to exist, let alone thrive. Improvements and innovation tend to be viewed as events, rather than ongoing processes.

Epilogue

Whether you have identified yourself as a Rudolph or not, we recognize that not everyone is going to become a Rudolph after reading the book. However, the tenets and thinking revealed should certainly help unearth your own latent Rudolphness and generate greater employee engagement as a result. We leave you with the challenge to go forth with your new awareness and thinking along with new ideas and tools to find those bright lights that drive innovation in your business. Identify the Rudolph within yourself and among your peers, nurture their distinctive needs, and build a team-based Rudolph Culture. Remember a Rudolph Culture is only sustainable when integrated with all Four Pillars of Organizational Greatness (including redefining leadership, developing a Corporate Constitution, and aligning the reward structure). Create your own unique sustainable competitive advantage by leveraging your Rudolph Factor ... and, as we heard them exclaim as we drove away from their site: "Enjoy the Journey!"

What did you think we were going to say?

"Happy Rudolph to all, and to all a good night!"

That, too!

RESOURCES

Books

Crother, Cyndi. *Catch! A Fishmonger's Guide to Greatness*, San Francisco, CA: Berrett-Koehler Publishing, 2003.

Deming, W. Edwards. *The New Economics*. 2nd ed. Cambridge, MA: MIT Press, 2000.

Johnson, H. Thomas, and Anders Broms. *Profit Beyond Measure*, New York: Free Press, 2000.

Spong, E. David, and Debbie J. Collard. *The Making of a World-Class Organization*, Milwaukee, WI: ASQ Quality Press, 2008.

Networks

The In2:InThinking Network
www.in2in.org

Pegasus Communications
www.pegasuscom.com

The Deming Cooperative
www.deming.edu

Web Sites and Quality Related Associations

Guide to Greatness, LLC
www.guidetogreatness.com

Rudolph Factor
www.rudolphfactor.com

Baldrige National Quality Program
www.quality.nist.gov

American Society for Quality
www.asq.org

American Society of Training and Development
www.astd.org

California Council for Excellence
www.calexcellence.org

Center for Organizational Excellence Research
www.coer.org.nz

INDEX

INDEX

ABOUT THE AUTHORS

Cyndi Laurin, PhD, is founder of Guide to Greatness, LLC, author of *Catch! A Fishmonger's Guide to Greatness*, an international speaker, and a business developer. Cyndi Laurin is passionate about provoking an awareness of thinking in individuals and organizations. Cyndi believes a collective awareness of our thought and language is the proverbial *silver bullet* to organizational greatness. Her insights and expertise in process improvement and performance excellence are transforming both domestic and international organizations. Cyndi Laurin taught for 10 years in the College of Business at California Polytechnic State University, San Luis Obispo, and has also taught for The National Graduate School of Quality Management and California State University, Dominguez Hills, in the areas of quality systems management.

Cyndi Laurin's degrees include a BS in Industrial Technology from California Polytechnic State University, San Luis Obispo (1992); an MA in Industrial and

Technical Studies from California Polytechnic State University, San Luis Obispo (1994); an MA in Educational Leadership and Organizations from the University of California, Santa Barbara (1995); and a PhD in Educational Leadership and Organizations from the University of California, Santa Barbara (1997). Her areas of expertise are process improvement, performance management, leadership development, corporate training, and team dynamics. She was awarded the Distinguished Educator of the Year in 2001–2001 by the California Faculty Association, California Polytechnic State University, San Luis Obispo.

Dr. Laurin lives by the tenets she presents to thousands of people every year, and she firmly believes that greatness (or having an extraordinary life) is generated from within. She believes it is possible for anyone to live an extraordinary life, and from her commitment to the success of people and organizations, she intends to focus her life's work encouraging and facilitating others' journeys in paving their own roads to greatness.

Craig Morningstar is a COO of a financial service firm in Arizona. He is an experienced business leader with a unique ability to quickly discover, elevate, and execute on business opportunities that many people do not see. This skill set of seeing problems and opportunities—where others do not—works to compliment senior management teams, boards, and advisory boards that are focused on goals, problems, opportunities, and competition.

Craig's background includes eight years at Southwest Airlines and eight years at Charles Schwab in addition to starting, owning, operating, growing, and selling companies. His business leadership and board experiences include law, accounting and financial firms, software, medical services, transportation, shipping, business services, and a variety of franchise companies.

In addition to leadership and board positions with for-profit companies, he has extensive experience with nonprofit organizations in leadership and mentoring roles and is active throughout the year with speaking engagements.

He holds multiple certifications and licenses in the quality, finance, compliance, and aero industry. He is a regular participant of various industry professional boards and associations.